Essential CSS & DHTML
for Web Professionals

ISBN 0-13-012760-4

90000

9 780130 127600

Other Books in the Series

- *Essential Perl 5 for Web Professionals*
  Micah Brown, Chris Bellew, and Dan Livingston

- *Essential Photoshop 5 for Web Professionals*
  Brad Eigen, Dan Livingston, and Micah Brown

- *Essential JavaScript for Web Professionals*
  Dan Barrett, Dan Livingston, and Micah Brown

Essential CSS & DHTML for Web Professionals

Dan Livingston
Wire Man Productions

Micah Brown
Etail Enterprises

Prentice Hall PTR
Upper Saddle River, NJ 07458
http://www.phptr.com

Library of Congress Cataloging-in-Publication Data

Livingston, Dan.
    Essential CSS & DHTML for Web professionals / Dan Livingston, Micah Brown.
        p. cm -- (Prentice Hall essential Web professionals series)
    ISBN 0-13-012760-4 (pbk.)
    1. DHTML (Document markup language) 2. Web sites--Design.
I. Brown, Micah. II. Title. III. Series.
QA76.76.H94L58   1999
005.7'2--dc21   99-32973
                                                    CIP

Editorial/Production Supervision: Benchmark Productions, Inc.
Acquisitions Editor: Karen McLean
Cover Design Director: Jerry Votta
Cover Design: Scott Weiss
Cover Illustration: Jean Francois Podevin, from *The Stock Illustration Source, Vol. 5*
Manufacturing Manager: Alexis R. Heydt
Editorial Assistant: Audri Anna Bazlen
Marketing Manager: Dan Rush
Project Coordinator: Anne Trowbridge

Prentice Hall books are widely used by corporations and government agencies for training, marketing, and resale.

The publisher offers discounts on this book when ordered in bulk quantities. For more information, contact: Corporate Sales Department, Phone: 800-382-3419; Fax: 201-236-7141; E-mail: corpsales@prenhall.com; or write: Prentice Hall PTR, Corp. Sales Dept., One Lake Street, Upper Saddle River, NJ 07458.

Printed in the United States of America

10 9 8 7 6 5 4 3 2

ISBN 0-13-012760-4

Prentice-Hall International (UK) Limited, *London*
Prentice-Hall of Australia Pty. Limited, *Sydney*
Prentice-Hall Canada Inc., *Toronto*
Prentice-Hall Hispanoamericana, S.A., *Mexico*
Prentice-Hall of India Private Limited, *New Delhi*
Prentice-Hall of Japan, Inc., *Tokyo*
Prentice-Hall (Singapore) Pte. Ltd., *Singapore*
Editora Prentice-Hall do Brasil, Ltda., *Rio de Janeiro*

Contents

Introduction   ix

Acknowledgments   xv

About the Authors   xvii

Chapter 1   Stylesheet Fundamentals   1

The Big Projects   1

Task: Lay Out the Shelley Homepage in
  Cascading Style Sheets (CSS)   1

Positioning Elements   2
  Defining Position with `<STYLE>`   2
  Blocking Off Content with `<DIV>`   5
  Stacking with Z-index   6

Adding Style to Elements   8
  Modifying HTML Tags   8

Classes   12
  Tight Control with `<SPAN>`   16
  Cascading and Overlapping   16
  ID Selectors   17

Chapter 2   The DHTML Begins   19

Task: Add DHTML Interactivity to the Shelley
Homepage   19

Pop-up Search Window   20

Using JavaScript to Pop Up Secondary
Navigation   24

Cycling through a Feature Splash Screen   27

Chapter 3   Cross-Browser Coding   33

Task: Code the DHTML on the Shelley Homepage
to Be Cross-Browser   33

Coding for Both Browsers Using the `eval()`
Statement   34

Coding for Layer Visibility   35

Browser-Specific Features to Avoid   36

Chapter 4   Preparing a Storefront for DHTML   37

The Big Project   37

Task: Preparing the *Stitch* Page for
E-Commerce   38

Overview of the Storefront   39

Setting Up CSS and JavaScript   42

Chapter 5   Animating Layers   49

Task: Create Animated Product Rollout for Three
Product Lines   49

Animate a Single Layer   50

Animate Multiple Layers   52

Another Method   54

Chapter 6   Dragging Layers   57

Task: Create Draggable Layers for Placing Products
in the Shopping Cart   57

How the Code Works   58

Events   58

Browser Differences   61

Objects 61
Dragging and User Interface 62
Clipping Regions 64
The Meat of the Code 65
What We Left Out 73

Chapter 7   A Really Interactive Quiz: Part One 75
Task: Create a Fully Interactive Quiz for Shelley
   Biotechnologies 75
The Functional Spec 76
   The Quiz Questions 77
   Scoring 77
   Progress/Navigation 77
   After the Quiz 78
Building the Questions 78
Cycling through the Questions 83

Chapter 8   A Really Interactive Quiz: Part Two 99
Introduction 99
Quiz Progress and Navigation 100
   What Should Happen 100
   Quiz Progress Images and Code 102
   The End of the Quiz 106

Appendix A   CSS Style Attribute Reference 111

Appendix B   Miscellaneous Reference 133

Appendix C   JavaScript Reference 137

Appendix D   Cross-Browser DOM Reference 171

Index 215

Introduction

When we first started learning DHTML, there were two kinds of books on the market: overly simplified, cutesy books that were appropriate for technophobic junior high schoolers; and huge reference tomes that could be used to prop up a house. But nothing actually taught us to build pages for real clients using stylesheets and DHTML.

This book will guide you through stylesheets and DHTML using examples taken straight from our experience as Web designers and programmers. We'll start off with basic concepts and simple examples and work up to some pretty sophisticated effects and functionality.

Now let's look at how this book is laid out and what DHTML can and can't do.

◆ How This Book Is Laid Out

Most of us learn how to create content for the Web when we're forced to. Your boss was maybe impressed by something fancy another CEO showed her, and since you helped her with her e-mail once, you're the resident expert in all things Web. She wants you to implement some "DHTML stuff" on your company's Web site. You say, "No problem." You think, "OK, I have something to learn now."

In our everyday lives this is often the way in which we expand our skills: We are given a job and if we don't know exactly how to do it, then we quickly learn how. In writing this book we decided to parallel the real world: This book is split into two main projects, and for each main project we will be responsible for the creation and/or upgrading of Web sites for two fictitious companies.

In the first three chapters of the book we will be using DHTML to create the homepage for Shelley Biotechnologies, a fast-growing biotech startup. In each chapter we will have at least one subproject that will consist of commonly used DHTML. We'll keep the difficulty down and focus on the DHTML you'll need to know first. At the end of each chapter, there will be more advanced exercises that you can complete on your own to expand your skills.

In the second half of the book we'll be creating an interactive storefront for *Stitch Magazine's* first foray into e-commerce. These tasks are more advanced than those found in the first project and will show you some of the powerful things you can do using DHTML.

The exercises in the chapters are designed to give you a solid foundation in DHTML, as well as many advanced skills and techniques that will carry you through the vast majority of DHTML projects you'll encounter. You will find that more often than not there is more than one way to do things in DHTML. There really aren't right and wrong ways to accomplish tasks.

For all of the examples in the book you will be able to go to the companion Web site located at http://www.phptr .com/essential and download the HTML and images needed to follow along with the exercises.

◆ An Introduction to DHTML

Before jumping straight into the code, let's look at DHTML and get an idea of what it is, how it's implemented by different browsers, and what it can and can't do. Then we'll jump into the code.

What Is DHTML?

DHTML stands for "Dynamic HTML," but in reality it's just using JavaScript and stylesheets together. That's it. It's easy to get a grander idea from the name: People often use the phrase "dynamically generated Web pages" to refer to Web pages that are created on the fly. The "Dynamic" in DHTML just means, "Wow, it moves around."

DHTML is still very powerful. It allows you to create effects that were impossible with plain HTML and JavaScript. The stylesheets (the official name is Cascading Style Sheets, or CSS) also let you position elements on the screen exactly where you want them without having to wrangle tables in HTML.

For those of you who are new to the world of Web development and are maybe learning JavaScript in conjunction with HTML, a quick rundown of what JavaScript is may be in order. JavaScript is Netscape's built-in scripting language, which is cross-platform so it will work on all platforms just like HTML. JavaScript allows you to enhance the functionality of your Web pages by embedding applications into your HTML. You can use JavaScript to build applications that range from adding interactivity to your pages to applications that interact with databases. Although Netscape created JavaScript, it will work on most modern browsers, including Microsoft's Internet Explorer. JavaScript isn't directly supported in Microsoft's Internet Explorer; IE does, however, have its own scripting language called JScript that supports most of the features found in JavaScript. The few instances in which the languages differ will be pointed out and a work-around will be presented.

There are two methods that you can use to include JavaScript in your Web pages—client-side and server-side. Both methods share the same basic language sets. This core language defines a base set of objects and features that will work in both client-side and server-side applications. Both methods also have extended object and feature sets that apply only to them.

Browsers and Versions

DHTML can only be viewed on version 4.0 and later of Microsoft's Internet Explorer and Netscape's Navigator. If you try to view a page written in DHTML with a 3.x browser, more likely than not you'll see a page with all of the images lined up in a straight vertical line down the page. And since, by the latest counts, 20%–40% of surfers are still using older browsers, you'll probably have to create two different Web pages: a standard HTML version and a DHTML version. For this reason, DHTML has not exploded onto the Web development scene.

Predictably, the two browsers differ somewhat in their implementation of DHTML. This isn't entirely their fault, though: They were released before the DHTML standards were set. Netscape Navigator 4.0 was released long before Microsoft's IE4, and thus had less of a firm direction as far as which standards would be included and which ones would be trashed. Doing the same thing in both browsers often requires separate code (we'll cover this in Chapter 3). Both browsers also include a host of proprietary tags and functions that only work on that browser. We'll tell you what they are and we'll also tell you to ignore these tags completely.

The upshot of all this is that you have to write your DHTML carefully and make sure you test your Web pages thoroughly. That means on both Mac and PC, MSIE and Netscape. It's a pain, but if you want to create something solid and professional, it's what you do.

A word about JavaScript: Netscape created Java-Script a while ago and, technically, MSIE doesn't support it. However, Microsoft does have its *own* language called JScript, which has many, many similarities to JavaScript. And, of course, neither language has anything at all to do with Java.

What DHTML Can and Can't Do

While the applications that you can create using DHTML are really only limited by your imagination, there are several things you cannot do, such as accessing or controlling the user's machine. For security reasons, writing to a user's computer is severely limited. You can store data on the user's machine only through the use of a cookie, and even then you are limited to a simple text file. This protects users from scripts that might do their computers harm or allow unscrupulous programmers from accessing personal information.

And, of course, you're still limited by bandwidth and how fast the browser operates. In a perfect world, you could create massive, gorgeous images that flow and swoop smoothly across the computer screen. We're not there yet, but we're getting there. (Future hint: Learn the Web because it's great technology that's only going to get bigger, but start looking at video closely. The next few generations of computers and software will create a desktop video production revolution similar to the desktop publishing revolution the Mac ushered in 15 years ago.)

With all that in mind, let's start looking at DHTML. There's some juicy stuff here, so have fun!

Acknowledgments

◆ Dan Livingston

We had the good luck to work with Mark Taub and Karen McLean from Prentice Hall on this project. We especially tested Karen's cattle-herding skills, and she remained remarkably patient and focused throughout the process.

I would like to thank my fiancée, Tanya Muller, for her continuing patience and encouragement. I wouldn't have been able to write this book while starting my own business without her by my side. Her support was, and continues to be, invaluable.

I'd also like to thank W. Bradley Scott of Clear Ink for coming up with the idea of using an online fashion magazine as a fictional company. He also acted as technical reviewer, and was generally very helpful.

Finally, I'd like to thank my design mentor, Brad Eigen of MadBoy Productions. He's the Daddy.

◆ Micah Brown

I would like to give special thanks to my wife, Dawn, who has helped me in too many ways to mention. You are my love, my life, and most importantly, my best friend. I dedicate this book to her and our daughter, Ashley Nova, who has yet to be born into this world—we can't wait to meet you!

Also a special thanks to my parents, William and Donna, and my extended parents, Beppe and Joy, for everything they have done for me these last 29 years, I wouldn't be the person I am today if it weren't for them. I will always be grateful for how much you all have taught me through the years and helped me to grow as a person.

Thanks to Mark Taub and Karen McLean for helping Dan and me get this book series out of our brains and onto paper. You are right, this is a little tougher than we had first imagined! Also, thanks to Carl Gorman, my partner in crime at Etail Enterprises (www.etail.com), and my band members, Kelly and Carl from Nitrus, for putting up with me through all of this.

Finally, thanks to my co-author Dan Livingston, as well as all the others who worked on the books in this series. If it weren't for you, I wouldn't be writing this.

About the Authors

◆ Dan Livingston

Coming from a background in marine biology, Dan Livingston was drawn to Web design in early 1996. His Web sites have since included high-profile clients such as Apple, Pacific Bell, and Novell. His sites have won numerous awards, and have been featured both in design books and on *CNN Prime Time*. His envelope-pushing DHTML site, Palette Man, has received international recognition, as well as "Cool Site" awards from Yahoo!, Macromedia, and *USA Today*. Dan was a Web designer and scripter at the Web design firm Clear Ink before starting his own successful design/user interface company, Wire Man Productions. He continues to produce titles for Prentice Hall's *Essential* series.

◆ Micah Brown

After working in the print industry for several years, Micah Brown started his career with the Web industry back in 1995 as both a programmer and designer. Some of the sites Micah has under his belt are Dr. Laura, Pacific Bell, Amazing Discoveries, and Ascend Communications.

Micah has also been a technical reviewer for Prentice Hall for the last three years for various publications, most notably *Perl by Example* by Ellie Quigley.

Micah is currently a co-owner of Etail Enterprises, a Web consulting firm located in southern California that specializes in bringing companies into this new arena of online advertising.

1 Stylesheet Fundamentals

IN THIS CHAPTER

- The Big Projects
- Task: Lay Out the Shelley Homepage in Cascading Style Sheets (CSS)
- Positioning Elements
- Adding Style to Elements
- Classes
- Recap
- Advanced Projects

◆ The Big Projects

We're going to learn Cascading Style Sheets ("stylesheets") and DHTML through the course of completing two fairly large, real-world-based projects. The first big project will be creating the home-page of a fictional company, Shelley Biotechnologies, Inc., in stylesheets and then adding some serious interactivity with DHTML.

◆ Task: Lay Out the Shelley Homepage in Cascading Style Sheets (CSS)

In this chapter, we're going to use stylesheets to create the home-page for Shelley Biotechnologies, Inc. First, we'll position all the elements of the page; in other words, all the text and images, exactly where we want them using <STYLE> and <DIV> tags. Then we'll modify some HTML tags so they better suit our purposes. These two uses—positioning elements and modifying HTML tag definitions—are what stylesheets are really good for.

◆ Positioning Elements

The ability to place images and blocks of text exactly where and how you want them is one of the most important advantages of CSS. It allows you to design a page with the kind of precision and control that used to be reserved for print designers. You still have to worry about download time, but the ability to position elements on your Web page is a wonderful thing.

Defining Position with <STYLE>

The Shelley Biotech homepage appears as shown in Figure 1–1.

FIGURE 1–1 The Shelley Biotechnologies homepage

The images we'll be using to create the pages in stylesheets are slightly different than the ones that would be used in a non-stylesheet layout. The images we'll be using are shown in Figures 1–2 through 1–6.

Shelley Biotechnologies, Inc.

FIGURE 1–2 company_name.gif

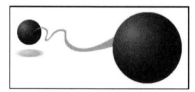

FIGURE 1–3 logo.jpg

FIGURE 1–4 main_nav.gif

FIGURE 1–5 resource_nav.gif

Here's how to place the company name (header.gif) at a specific location on the page using stylesheets:

```
<HTML>
<HEAD>
<TITLE>Welcome to Shelley Biotechnologies, Inc.</TITLE>
```

1.  ```
    <STYLE TYPE="text/css">
    ```

2.  ```
    #companyName
    {
        position: absolute;
    ```

FIGURE 1–6 feature.gif

```
        top: 20px;
        left: 20px;
}

</STYLE>

</HEAD>

<BODY BGCOLOR="#FFFFFF">

...

</BODY>
</HTML>
```

HOW THE CODE WORKS

1. All the styles and layers of the Web page are declared inside the `<STYLE>` and `</STYLE>` tags. A *layer* can contain any chunk of HTML, including text, tables, images, links, and even forms. A *style* is a modification of an HTML tag. Using the words style and layer in this manner isn't technically correct, but it's how the majority of Web designers use the terms.

2. We're declaring a layer called `companyName`. The `#` means the contents of the layer are spelled out somewhere else in the document, much like intradocument links in regular HTML (for example, `<A HREF="#top">`).

`position: absolute` means that we're going to tell the layer exactly where it's supposed to go. The other option is `position: relative`, which tells the layer to simply position itself wherever it happens to fall.

`top: 20px` and `left: 20px` tells the browser to position this layer 20 pixels over from the left edge of the browser window and 20 pixels down from the top edge of the browser window.

It's vital that you place all the information about layers inside curly braces {}, and end each line with a semicolon. If there's trouble with your code, always check your curly braces and semicolons—new programmers often forget them.

Blocking Off Content with <DIV>

We determine the content of `companyName` inside the `<BODY>` of the page.

```
<BODY BGCOLOR="#FFFFFF">

<DIV ID="companyName">
<IMG SRC="images/home/company_name.gif" HEIGHT="128"
WIDTH="428" ALT="Shelley Biotechnologies, Inc.">
</DIV>

</BODY>
```

The `<DIV>` tag with an `ID=name` attribute contains everything that goes in a certain layer. Here, we're determining the content of the layer `companyName`. The only thing in this layer is a single image.

Here's the code for the rest of the layers:

```
#logo { position: absolute; top: 9px; left: 304px; }
#mainNavigation { position: absolute; top: 138px; left:
25px; }
#resourceNavigation { position: absolute; top: 173px;
left: 189px; }
#feature { position: absolute; top: 194px; left: 19px; }
#companyName { position: absolute; top: 16px; left:
29px; }
```

Notice a layer's information can be on the same line as long as there are semicolons between the attributes. The content of these layers is determined inside the <BODY>. We're not going to spell out every line of HTML—we just want you to get a general idea.

```
<DIV ID="companyName">
<IMG SRC="images/company_name.gif" ALT="Shelley
Biotechnologies, Inc." WIDTH="426" HEIGHT="126"
BORDER="0">
</DIV>

<DIV ID="logo">
<IMG SRC="images/logo.jpg" "Shelley Logo" WIDTH="275"
HEIGHT="117" BORDER="0">
</DIV>

<DIV ID="mainNavigation">
<IMG SRC="images/main_nav.gif" "Main Navigation"
WIDTH="561" HEIGHT="42" BORDER="0" USEMAP="#mainnav">
</DIV>

<DIV ID="resourceNavigation">
<IMG SRC="images/resource_nav.gif" ALT="Resource
Navigation" WIDTH="396" HEIGHT="31" BORDER="0"
USEMAP="#resnav">
</DIV>

<DIV ID="feature">
<IMG SRC="images/feature_1.gif" ALT="Salsa!"
WIDTH="571" HEIGHT="299" BORDER="0" USEMAP="#feature">
</DIV>
```

Figure 1–7 shows you what the homepage looks like.

Whoops. Some of the images are overlapping others, so we're not done yet. Let's look at what's happening and why.

Stacking with Z-index

Both browsers stack layers according to where the layer occurs in the code. Layers that occur first (such as companyName) are placed on the bottom, and layers that occur later in the code (such as logo) are displayed on top of whatever's already there. Thus, the image of the logo is above the company name, so it overlaps and hides part of the Shelley Biotechnologies image. There are two ways to get around this: 1) Make the top image transparent so the bottom image shows through. But that won't work here because the logo is a JPEG, and you can't get transparency out of a JPEG.

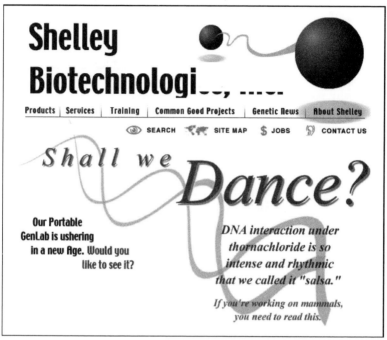

FIGURE 1–7 Screen shot of Shelley Biotech's homepage

Therefore, you have to 2) change the layer stacking order using something new called the z-index.

```
#companyName
{
    z-index: 1;
    position: absolute;
    top: 20px;
    left: 20px;
}
```

The z-index tells the browser which layer is on top. If you don't say which z-index a layer is, it's assumed to be on a z-index of zero, and the browser stacks the layers according to their order in the code.

So, in this case, company_name.gif needs its whitespace to be transparent or we get the same problem we did when logo.jpg was on top: The upper image overlaps and hides the one below it.

SOMETHING THAT WILL TRIP YOU UP LATER

You'll notice for feature.gif we included the "ushering in a new age" text in the image. You may have wondered why we didn't just make the "ushering" text another layer and put it on top of the "Shall We Dance?" image. There's a good reason for this: If they were on separate layers, the links wouldn't have worked.

If you have two overlapping layers and there are clickable images on both those layers, only the images on the top layer will be automatically clickable. The browser simply won't see the clickable images on the lower layer, and nothing will happen when you click on them. This is true even if the clickable images aren't directly underneath the layer above them. There's a way to work around it, but it involves some pretty fancy DHTML. We'll be covering that specific technique in Chapter 7, "A Really Interactive Quiz: Part One."

Stylesheets are great for precisely positioning elements on your page, allowing you greater design freedom and easier layout (no more tables!).

◆ Adding Style to Elements

The other major advantage of stylesheets is being able to modify HTML tags so they do exactly what you want them to. Your control over these tags can be over individual tags, like <B> or <H1>, or you can create whole classes of formatting rules that can apply to many tags.

Modifying HTML Tags

Generally, the only modifications you can make to HTML tags are changes to how those tags display text. You can't create new tags or make tags do something totally different, such as making a <FORM> tag display an image.

We're going to alter the anchor tag <A>, the bold tag <B>, and the italic tag <I>.

```
<STYLE TYPE="text/css">

...[ your layer declarations would go here ]...
```

1. `A { text-decoration: none; }`

2. `B { font-size: 10pt; font-family: verdana, sans-serif; }`

3. `I { font-size: 9 pt; font-color: #333333; font-family: verdana, sans-serif; }`

`</STYLE>`

HOW THE CODE WORKS

1. Look at `A { text-decoration: none; }`. In the world of stylesheets, text decorations are the underlines on hyperlinks, so this line of code tells the user's browser to not display the underlines in links.

2. Now look at `B { font-size...}`. This line modifies the `<B>` tag to not only make text bold, but also to make the font size 10 points, and to display it in the Verdana font. If the visitor doesn't have Verdana, the browser will use the default sans-serif font (usually Arial for PC users or Helvetica for Mac users) on the visitor's system.

3. The last tag modification is what we do to the `<I>` tag. We shrink the text size to 9 points, change the text color to dark gray (#333333), and display the text in Verdana or the user's sans-serif font face.

These are the only tag modifications we'll be using for this example, but there are over a hundred different ways to define a tag. Here are a few examples:

```
color: red;
font-weight: bold;
font-style: italic;
line-spacing: 24pt;
```

The rest of the modifications you're supposed to be able to use are available in Appendix A, "CSS Style Attribute Reference." However, different browsers support different modifications, so test your code on both the Internet Explorer (IE) and Netscape browsers before committing to them.

Be wary of using color names like we did with `color: red`. You can never be completely sure of how a named color will look on a user's browser. With named colors, the browser decides what color "red" is and displays its own version of red. For colors like black, white, red, and blue, you'll get similar colors across browsers, but be careful if you get fancy with colors like "coral." It's always safest to use hex values; for example, `color: #FF0000`. We're using named colors here for simplicity's sake.

To put these modifications to work, we'll first add a layer for the text links and copyright information:

```
#text
{
     position: absolute;
     top: 200px;
     left: 10px;
}
```

and then we'll fill out the following layer:

```
<DIV ID="text">
<CENTER>


<P CLASS="superBig">
<A HREF="products/index.html">Products</A>  |
<A HREF="services/index.html">Services</A>  |
<A HREF="training/index.html">Training</A><BR>
<A HREF="commongood/index.html">Common Good Projects</A>  |
<A HREF="news/index.html">Genetic News</A>  |
<A HREF="about/index.html">About Shelley</A>
</P>

<P CLASS="green">
<A HREF="search/index.html">Search</A>  |
<A HREF="sitemap.html">Site Map</A>  |
<A HREF="jobs/index.html">Jobs</A>  |
<A HREF="contact/index.html">Contact Us</A>
</P>

<P CLASS="copyright">
&copy; 1999 shelley biotechnologies, inc. all rights
reserved.
</P>

</CENTER>
</DIV>
```

You'll notice we included a `</P>` tag, which you almost never see in plain HTML. However, when you're using stylesheets, you should close your `<P>` tags. You'll see why this is useful in the next section, "Classes."

ABOUT RENDERED FONTS

You may have heard about being able to use any font you want on a Web page using stylesheets. This is true, but there's a catch: You have to use TrueDoc with Netscape (which costs you money for every font you use), or use OpenType with IE. There isn't a system that works in both browsers. So our advice is to forget both of these systems—it's not worth the money or the headache to deal with both of them. If you absolutely have to use a certain font, use an image or a small Flash movie (our forthcoming book on Flash is a great resource).

Our Shelley homepage is laid out correctly and appears as shown in Figure 1–8.

FIGURE 1–8 The new and improved homepage

There is another way to modify your HTML tags. You can put the style directly into the tag itself without having to define it earlier in the code. It isn't used very often and we don't recommend it, because overuse of this technique can make your code very hard to follow, especially when there's a style error and you can't find where it's coming from. Here's an example:

```
<BODY>
<!-- text that's big, red, and arial -->
<H1 STYLE="color:red; font-size:24pt; font-
family:arial;">
Shelley Biotechnologies
</H1>

<!-- regular H1 text -->
<H1>Bringing Biotech into the Home (not red)</H1>
</BODY>
```

◆ Classes

Classes are another way to determine how the text on your page looks. Essentially, you're determining a set of styles such as color, font weight, font size, and so on, but you're not assigning it to any particular tag. Here's what a class looks like:

```
<STYLE TYPE="text/css">

<!-- layer declarations -->

#text
{
      position: absolute;
      top: 400px;
      left: 10px;
}

<!-- tag modifications -->

A { text-decoration: none; }

<!-- classes -->

.regular
{
      color: red;
}

.superBig
```

```
{
     font-size: 16pt;
     font-weight: bold;
     color: red;
}

.copyright
{
     font-size: 9pt;
     font-style: italic;
     text-transform: capitalize;
}

</STYLE>
```

We've created three classes here: regular, superBig, and copyright. Here's how we could implement these classes in the text navigation layer we looked at earlier.

```
<DIV ID="text">
<CENTER>


<P CLASS="superBig">
<A HREF="products/index.html">Products</A> |
<A HREF="services/index.html">Services</A> |
<A HREF="training/index.html">Training</A><BR>
<A HREF="commongood/index.html">Common Good Projects</A> |
<A HREF="news/index.html">Genetic News</A> |
<A HREF="about/index.html">About Shelley</A>
</P>

<P CLASS="regular">
<A HREF="search/index.html">Search</A> |
<A HREF="sitemap.html">Site Map</A> |
<A HREF="jobs/index.html">Jobs</A> |
<A HREF="contact/index.html">Contact Us</A>
</P>

<P CLASS="copyright">
&copy; 1999 shelley biotechnologies, inc. all rights
reserved.
</P>

</CENTER>
</DIV>
```

See where we're applying the classes? All of the text in the first line of links will be big and bold text, any nonlinked text will be red, the bottom row of links is smaller, and the copyright information is smaller still, italicized, and the first letter of every word is capitalized (see Figure 1–9).

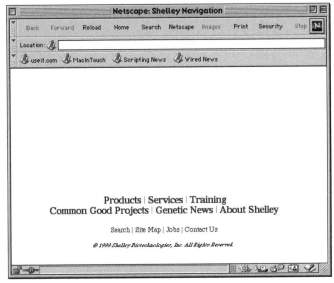

FIGURE 1–9 The altered links using the superBig, regular, and copyright classes

You can also specifically bind a class to a tag. For example:

```
P
{
font-weight: bold;
font-size: 12pt;
font-family: verdana, sans-serif;
}

P.small
{
font-size: 9pt;
margin-left: 5em;
margin-right; 5em;
}
```

Here's how to apply the class:

```
<P>
Shelley Biotechnologies is the uncontested leader in
affordable biotechnology products.
</P>

<P CLASS="small">
How often does a company get to say that they don't have
any competition? (No, the military doesn't count.)
</P>
```

Notice that the 9-point font size in the P.small class over-rides the 12-point font size in the regular <P> tag.

Now, let's add a nontag-specific class to the mix:

```
.cool { color: blue; font-style: italic; }
```

and create some code that looks like this:

```
<DIV CLASS="cool">

<P>
Shelley Biotechnologies is the uncontested leader in
affordable biotechnology products.
</P>

<P CLASS="small">
How often does a company get to say that they don't have
any competition? (No, the military doesn't count.)
</P>

</DIV>
```

All of the text in the two paragraphs will be blue and italicized. The first paragraph will be blue, italicized, bold, 12-point, and in Verdana. The second paragraph will be blue, italicized, have wide margins, and be 9 points in size.

You can't directly combine classes, or include two classes in one definition. For example, this would never work:

```
<P CLASS="small,cool">
```

So what do you do when you want to apply two classes at once? You use the <SPAN> tag.

Tight Control with <SPAN>

The <SPAN> tag is a nice, all-purpose tool to apply style whenever you feel like it. Say we're still using the styles and classes we discussed earlier.

```
<P CLASS="small">
Shelley Biotechnologies is a family-oriented company -
<SPAN CLASS="cool">safety is extremely important to us
</SPAN>, which is why we require a one-week training
period before anyone is allowed to use our flagship
product, the Portable BioLab.
</P>
```

<SPAN> doesn't do anything except apply the class cool to the phrase safety is extremely important to us. If you wanted to apply the classes small and cool to the entire paragraph, you could do this:

```
<P CLASS="small"><SPAN CLASS="cool">
Shelley Biotechnologies is a family-oriented company -
safety is extremely important to us, which is why we
require a one-week training period before anyone is
allowed to use our flagship product, the Portable
BioLab.
</SPAN></P>
```

If you really wanted to go nuts, you could add a nested <SPAN> tag inside the paragraph.

```
<P CLASS="small"><SPAN CLASS="cool">
Shelley Biotechnologies is a family-oriented company -
<SPAN STYLE="font-weight: bold; font-size: 16pt;">safety
is extremely important to us</SPAN>, which is why we
require a one-week training period before anyone is
allowed to use our flagship product, the Portable
BioLab.
</SPAN></P>
```

You should also note that <SPAN CLASS="small"> should not be used before the small class is specifically bound to the <P> tag. Current browsers are generally forgiving enough to let you use tag-bound classes with other tags, but it's a bad habit to get into.

Cascading and Overlapping

We've talked a lot about the "Style Sheets" part of Cascading Style Sheets. Now we're going to look at what the "Cascading" means.

You've already seen cascading in action. When a <P> tag is defined to have a style, that style is carried through all the <P>s in the document. This style *cascades* down the page. If a <P> tag has a class assigned to it, the class styles apply everywhere inside that <P> tag. A mini-cascade occurs inside that <P> tag.

You've also seen several different ways a tag can have a style: from the actual stylesheet, from classes, and from styling directly inside the tag. This can result in several styles applying to a single tag. The way browsers deal with these overlapping styles is by deciding which styles are more important than others. In general, the more specific a style is, the greater importance it has. A Style attribute embedded in a tag is the ultimate specificity, and will thus override any rule. The least specific rules are the default ones set by the browsers; for example, using the Times font as the page's default font.

ID Selectors

An ID selector is similar to a class, but is much more limited. An ID selector can only be applied once in a document.

```
#specialOffer {font-family: gadget, serif; font-size:40;}
```

To call an ID selector:

```
<P CLASS="small" ID="specialOffer">
```

Due to their one-time-only use, ID selectors are rarely used. The only reason we've used them is for pure organization: It's helpful to have all your style information in a single place on your page. It keeps you from hunting all over your page looking for a single style.

RECAP

Congratulate yourself for making it here—that's a lot of learning in a few pages. You now know how to create layers in stylesheets and position them where you want to on the page, as well as layer them in the order you want. You also know how to modify HTML tags so text is displayed according to your design desires.

ADVANCED PROJECTS

Create a funky, swirling background in Photoshop (read our book, *Essential Photoshop 5 for Web Professionals*, if you don't know how). Then add some images of people to your background and have some of them overlap each other. Then chop the images up and use stylesheets to place these images on a Web page. The challenge is to create a Web page that looks exactly like your Photoshop document. Use precisely positioned layers to make everything match up.

2 The DHTML Begins

IN THIS CHAPTER

- Task: Add DHTML Interactivity to the Shelley Homepage
- Pop-up Search Window
- Using JavaScript to Pop Up Secondary Navigation
- Cycling through a Feature Splash Screen
- Recap
- Advanced Projects

◆ Task: Add DHTML Interactivity to the Shelley Homepage

Now that we've laid out the Shelley homepage in stylesheets, it's time to create something more interesting than a static home-page. We'll add some pop-up windows, change images within layers, and change whole layers. We do this with JavaScript. That's all DHTML is: stylesheets and JavaScript. DHTML stands for "Dynamic HTML," but don't get the "dynamic" confused with another popular term, "dynamically generated pages." Dynamically generated pages are Web pages that are assembled from various pieces by a Web server before being sent to your browser. The "Dynamic" in DHTML just means, "Wow, it moves around."

19

LIKE AN APPLICATION

DHTML will allow you to create Web pages and sites that act more like software applications than regular Web pages. We want you to think about this as you go forward learning DHTML—it's still new enough for almost anyone to create some true boundary-pushing work, including you.

◆ Pop-up Search Window

Let's say the Shelley Biotech Web site is huge: over 5000 pages and growing on a weekly basis. When visitors are confronted with a site as large as Shelley's, they'll often try to find some information via the site's search engine rather than trying to navigate through the site. To that end, let's make their searching a little easier: When they click on Search, we can send them to a separate search page, but it'd be quicker and more convenient to the visitor to pop up a small window that has a short HTML form and a Go Search button. To do this, we'll add the following code to our Shelley homepage:

```
<HTML>

...

<STYLE TYPE="text/css">

...

#search
{
    z-index: 5;
    position: absolute;
    top: 200px;
    left:400px;
    visibility: hidden;
}

</STYLE>

<SCRIPT LANGUAGE="javascript">
```

```
1.  function showLayer(layerName)
    {
        document.layers[layerName].visibility = 'visible'
    }

2.  function hideLayer(layerName)
    {
        document.layers[layerName].visibility = 'hidden'
    }
    </SCRIPT>

    ...

3.  <DIV ID="search">
    <H3>Search  the Shelley  Site</H3>
    <FORM ACTION="cgi-bin/search.pl" METHOD="post">
        <IMG SRC="images/search_hd.gif" ALT="Search"
        WIDTH="82" HEIGHT="15" BORDER="0">
        <P>
        <TABLE><TR>
           <TD VALIGN="middle"><INPUT TYPE="text"
           SIZE=30 NAME="searchString"></TD>
           <TD VALIGN="middle"><INPUT TYPE="image"
           SRC="images/search_go.gif" BORDER="0"></TD>
        </TD></TR></TABLE>
    </FORM>
    <P>
    <A HREF="javascript:hideLayer('search')">
    Close this window</A>
    </DIV>
```

HOW THE CODE WORKS

1. This is the code to change a layer's visibility in a Netscape browser. The code is slightly different for Internet Explorer (IE), but we'll look at that in the next chapter. For now, we're assuming you're using a Netscape browser.

2. It's the same to hide a layer; just swap `visible` with `hidden`.

3. Here's the HTML of the search layer—we're keeping it simple. We put the form elements in a table for formatting reasons—we want them to be vertically aligned along their middles. Note that we could also bring up another browser window using a `_blank` target, but the goal here is to enhance user experience by not forcing them to deal with extra windows.

The Search window appears as shown in Figure 2–1.

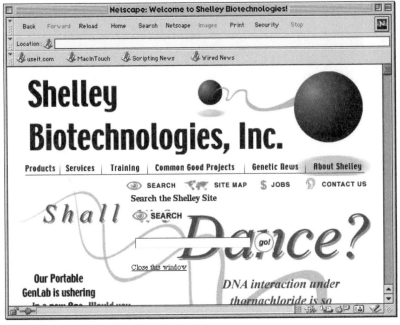

FIGURE 2–1 The Shelley Search window

Whoops. The layer below shows through, which doesn't look right. We want a solid background behind the Search layer. To add a white background, create a table with a background color, and put the navigation inside that table.

```
<DIV ID="search">
<TABLE BGCOLOR="#FFFFFF" CELLPADDING="10"><TR><TD>
    <H3>Search  the Shelley  Site</H3>
    <FORM ACTION="cgi-bin/search.pl" METHOD="post">
    Search for these keywords:<BR>
    <INPUT TYPE="text" SIZE="30" NAME="searchString">
    <P>
    <INPUT TYPE="image" SRC="images/
    search_button.gif"> BORDER="0">
    </FORM>
<P>
<A HREF="javascript:hideLayer('search')">
Close this window</A>
</TD></TR></TABLE>
</DIV>
```

Add the cellpadding to put a margin around the Search window to visually separate it from the layers below. Another way to separate this layer from surrounding layers is to add a border to it.

```
#search
{
    z-index: 5;
    position: absolute;
    top: 200px;
    left:400px;
    visibility: hidden;
}
```

Now it appears as shown in Figure 2–2.

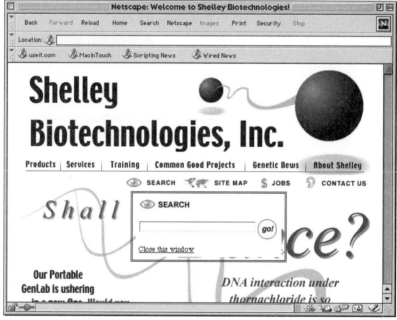

FIGURE 2–2 The corrected Shelley Search layer

Some of the layers below still peek through. This is hard to get rid of, so if you're in a hurry, you can increase the cellspacing (like we did) to turn this design bug into a design feature.

◆ Using JavaScript to Pop Up Secondary Navigation

Because the Shelley site is so large, designing its navigation is an interesting challenge. An easy way to improve user interface is to use DHTML to give the visitor more navigational information without taking up half the screen with links. We're going to modify the homepage navigation so that when someone clicks one of the main sections (Products, Training, and so on), a previously hidden layer with secondary navigation on it will appear.

Here's the additional Shelley homepage code to accomplish this:

```
<STYLE TYPE="text/css">

...

#productsNav {...}
#trainingNav {...}
#servicesNav {...}
#commongoodNav {...}
#newsNav {...}

</STYLE>

<SCRIPT LANGUAGE="javascript">


function showLayer(layerName)
{
     document.layers[layerName].visibility = 'visible'
}


function hideLayer(layerName)
{
     document.layers[layerName].visibility = 'hidden'
}
</SCRIPT>

...

<DIV ID="mainNavigation">
<IMG SRC=" /main_nav.gif" ALT="Main Navigation"
WIDTH="561" HEIGHT="42" BORDER="0" USEMAP="#mainnav">
<MAP NAME="mainnav">
```

```
        <AREA … HREF="javascript:showLayer('productsNav')">
        …
</MAP>
</DIV>

<DIV ID="productsNav">
<TABLE BGCOLOR="#FFFFFF" CELLPADDING=10><TR><TD>
<H3>Products</H3>
<A HREF="products/portable/">Portable BioLab</A><BR>
<A HREF="products/accessories/">Portable BioLab
Accessories</A><BR>
<A HREF="products/education/">Educational Products</A>
<BR>
<A HREF="products/corporate/">Corporate BioLabs</A><BR>
<A HREF="products/enterprise/">Enterprise BioLabs</A>
<P>
<A HREF="store/">How to order</A>
</P>
<P>
<A HREF="javascript:hideLayer('productsNav')">Close this
window</A>
</P>
</TD></TR></TABLE>
</DIV>

<DIV ID="trainingNav">
<TABLE BGCOLOR="#FFFFFF" CELLPADDING=10><TR><TD>
<H3>Training</H3>
<A HREF="training/begin/">Genetic Engineering for
Beginners</A><BR>
<A HREF="training/intermediate/">Intermediate Genetic
Engineering</A><BR>
<A HREF="training/advanced/">Advanced Genetic
Engineering</A><BR>
<A HREF="training/prof/">Professor Track Biogenesis</A>
<BR>
<A HREF="training/rdna/">rDNA Refresher Courses</A>
<P>
<A HREF="training/schedule.html">Build your training
schedule</A>
</P>
<P>
<A HREF="javascript:hideLayer('trainingNav')">Close this
window</A>
</P>
</TD></TR></TABLE>
</DIV>
```

You can download the code for the rest of the secondary navigation layers from our Web site at http://www.phptr.com/essential. Remember to add a table and background color.

Now, clicking on the other main sections (see Figure 2–3) . . .

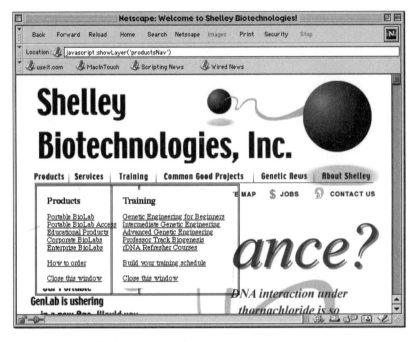

FIGURE 2–3 Multiple navigation layers

See the problem? We didn't include a way to hide the layers that we don't need. To fix this, we'll make JavaScript remember which navigation layer is visible. Then, when a visitor clicks on a new layer, we'll hide the old layer and show the new one, like so:

```
<SCRIPT LANGUAGE="javascript">
```

1.   `oldLayer = ""`

```
    function showNav(layerName)
    {
```

2.   `//hide the old layer`
       `if (oldLayer) // we need to make sure it's not`
       `{           // the visitor's 1`st` click`

```
            document.layers[oldLayer].visibility = 'hidden'
      }
```

3.     ```
       //make the correct layer visible
       document.layers[layername].visibility = 'visible'
       oldLayer = layerName
```
      }

### HOW THE CODE WORKS

1. `oldLayer` needs to be a global variable or JavaScript won't remember it from click to click. A global variable is one that's outside of a function. `oldLayer` will keep track of which layer is visible. Its initial value is nothing, because when a visitor first sees this page, no secondary navigation is visible.

2. If `oldLayer` doesn't have a value, that means that the visitor hasn't clicked on anything yet. Since there isn't a layer to hide, we can skip over the command to hide a layer. If there is an `oldLayer`, then that layer gets hidden.

3. We make the new layer visible and make that layer the `oldLayer`. When the visitor clicks on another link, this starts over again.

Now it works. In general, you should hide any old layer before making a new one visible because that decreases the chance the user will see both layers at the same time while the browser catches up with the code.

Making layers visible and invisible based on a visitor's clicking is probably what you'll be using DHTML for about 90% of the time.

## ◆ Cycling through a Feature Splash Screen

Let's add some splash to the homepage. We've got this big, eye-catching "Shall We Dance?" feature, so let's make it a little more interesting to really pull people in. To do this, we'll add two teaser screens to the "Shall We Dance?" feature along with an option to bypass the screens and go directly to the article's content.

We'll change the splash screen to look like the one that appears in Figure 2–4.

If visitors click "Full Story," they'll be shunted directly to the page where the article is. If they click "More," the "Shall We
```

FIGURE 2–4 Feature story with More and Full Story options

Dance?" image will be replaced by the second image in the teaser sequence (see Figure 2–5).

If they click "More" again, they'll be taken to the third and final image (see Figure 2–6).

Instead of swapping whole layers, let's just swap images within a layer.

```
<SCRIPT LANGUAGE="javascript">

    ...

1.  currentFeature = "1"

2.  function featureTeaser()
    {
        if ( currentFeature == "1" )
```

FIGURE 2–5 Second screen of the feature splash cycle

```
    {
        document.layers['feature'].images['teaser1'].src =
        'images/home/teaser2.gif'
        currentFeature = "2"
    }
    else if (currentFeature = "2")
    {
        document.layers['feature'].images['teaser1'].src =
        'images/home/teaser3.gif'
        currentFeature = "3"
    }
    else
    {
        location.href = "feature.html"
    }


...


<DIV ID="feature">
    <IMG SRC="images/home/feature.gif"  ALT="Shelley
    Biotechnologies, Inc." BORDER="0" USEMAP="#feature">
```

FIGURE 2–6 Final screen of the feature splash cycle

```
<MAP NAME="feature">
  <AREA SHAPE="rect" COORDS="500,300,582,323"
  HREF="javascript:featureTeaser()">
</MAP>
</DIV>
```

HOW THE CODE WORKS

1. As with the secondary navigation, we're setting a global variable to keep track of which image is visible. We initialize `currentFeature` to be 1 to indicate that the first feature image is visible to the site visitor.

2. In the `featureTeaser` function, we're changing the image based on the value of `currentFeature`. We add 1 to `currentFeature` each time we change the image so it loads a different image until it reaches 3. Once it reaches 3, we send the user to the full story with `location.href`.

You might have realized that we could have accomplished this same feat with a simple image replacement with HTML and JavaScript instead of using layers, because each layer is just an image. This is true in this case, but the goal is to teach you different techniques in DHTML, and some of your layers will have text on them, which can't be altered using JavaScript.

RECAP

We've learned how to display hidden layers, how to hide layers we don't want to see, and how to change images within certain layers even when the visitor is clicking in the same spot. We've covered the most popular use of DHTML in this chapter: displaying and hiding layers. The rest of the book adds some powerful functionality to what you've learned here, but you could build a decent DHTML site with what you know right now (well, after you've read how to code in different browsers in the next chapter).

ADVANCED PROJECTS

Create a Web page that acts like a software program. Create layers that look exactly like dialog boxes (the ones in regular software programs that have OK and Cancel buttons) and have those layers appear when visitors click on parts of your Web page, and call different JavaScript functions based on what button the visitors click. For example, by adding a script that displays numbers in a bunch of text boxes in a form, you could build your own Web-based spreadsheet.

3 Cross-Browser Coding

IN THIS CHAPTER

- Task: Code the DHTML on the Shelley Homepage to Be Cross-Browser
- Coding for Both Browsers Using the `eval()` Statement
- Coding for Layer Visibility
- Browser-Specific Features to Avoid
- Recap
- Advanced Projects

◆ Task: Code the DHTML on the Shelley Homepage to Be Cross-Browser

Netscape and Internet Explorer version 4 browsers implement DHTML differently: They need different JavaScript syntax to do the same thing. This is annoying but unavoidable. We have to code the Shelley homepage so both browsers can see and understand the DHTML.

Here's a browser difference that you'll be seeing the most:
In Netscape:

```
document.layers['search'].visibility = 'visible'
```

In IE:

```
document.all['search'].style.visibility = 'visible'
```

These two statements are close, but not close enough to work in the other's browser. Fortunately, you don't have to code two totally separate functions for each browser. There's an easier way, although it makes your code more difficult to read.

◆ Coding for Both Browsers Using the `eval()` Statement

The `eval()` method in JavaScript is the best way to code DHTML for both the Netscape and IE browsers at the same time. It does this by letting you dynamically generate your own JavaScript. Here's an example:

```
styleRef = ".style"
eval( "document.all.['bluething']." + styleRef +
".visibility = 'visible'")
```

The `eval()` method builds a string and then evaluates that string as if it were a regular command in JavaScript. In the first step of building this string, `eval()` takes whatever's between its parentheses.

```
"document.all.['bluething']." + styleRef +
".visibility = 'visible'"
```

After JavaScript inserts the values for `styleRef`, the string looks like:

```
"document.all['bluething'].style.visibility = 'visible'"
```

Next, `eval()` takes this string and tells JavaScript to execute this string as if it were a regular command. Thus, JavaScript executes the following command:

```
document.all['bluething'].style.visibility = 'visible'
```

and the layer `bluething` becomes visible, if you're using IE. Let's look at the code you'd actually put in your page.

◆ Coding for Layer Visibility

```
<SCRIPT LANGUAGE="JavaScript">
```

1. ```
   layerRef = ""
   styleRef = ""
   ```

2. ```
   if (navigator.appName == "Netscape")
   {
       layerRef = ".layers"
       styleRef = ""
   }
   else //must be IE
   {
       layerRef = ".all"
       styleRef = ".style"
   }
   ```

The preceding code should be in all of your pages that use DHTML, and it should come before all of the other JavaScript.

HOW THE CODE WORKS

1. These two variables, `layerRef` and `styleRef`, will be used in most of your DHTML code.

2. Notice that this `if` statement isn't in a function. That means it's run every time the page is loaded, which is what we want. We determine which browser the visitor is using and set `layerRef` and `styleRef` accordingly.

Further down in your script, you want to make the layer `productsNav` visible. Here's code that'll work in both browsers:

```
eval( "document" + layerRef  + "['findpants']" +
styleRef + ".visibility = 'visible'")
```

Note: You can use both single and double quotes in an `eval()` statement as long as you nest them. For example, we can switch the single and double quotes in the preceding example and the code will still work.

```
eval( 'document' + layerRef  + '["findpants"]' +
styleRef + '.visibility = "visible"')
```

However, if you try to mix single and double quotes indiscriminately, you'll get errors.

```
eval( 'document" + layerRef  + '['findpants']' +
styleRef + '.visibility = "visible'")
```

There's another way to code cross-browser DHTML that is more flexible, but takes longer. We'll cover this method later in the book.

◆ Browser-Specific Features to Avoid

We strongly recommend avoiding any features that are specific to one browser. No matter how cool the feature is, cutting off half your audience is not a good idea.

Netscape-only features to avoid:

1. `<layer>` tag

2. JavaScript Style Sheets

3. Bitstream fonts, also known as TrueDoc

IE 4.0-only features to avoid:

1. Direct Animation Controls

2. Data binding (tying into a database or text file on the Web server using ActiveX controls or Java applets)

3. VBScript (use only when it's an Active Server Page; for example, index.asp)

4. OpenType fonts

RECAP

This is a short but extremely important chapter. We've learned how to use the `eval()` statement to create DHTML that will work in Netscape's browser and in IE, which is the easiest way we know of to create cross-browser DHTML that works.

ADVANCED PROJECTS

Create the rest of the Shelley homepage using cross-browser coding techniques and the `eval()` statement.

4 Preparing a Storefront for DHTML

IN THIS CHAPTER

- The Big Project
- Task: Preparing the *Stitch* Page for E-Commerce
- Overview of the Storefront
- Setting Up CSS and JavaScript
- Recap
- Advanced Projects

◆ The Big Project

We're going to create the storefront for the e-commerce section of the *Stitch* Web site. *Stitch* is a fictional online fashion magazine. It covers fashion industry news and gossip, clothing trends both haute couture and street-level, profiles of designers and models, and daily columns. Small features are updated daily, while main features are updated weekly. The *Stitch* homepage appears in Figure 4–1.

Since *Stitch*'s marketing team has discovered that people interested in fashion also tend to buy more clothes than the average person, *Stitch* has decided to pump up its thin margin by selling a few products online—tee shirts, sweatshirts, mugs, and hats emblazoned with the *Stitch* logo.

FIGURE 4-1 The homepage for *Stitch*, a fictional online fashion magazine

A fleet of programmers is dealing with the complicated back end of the e-commerce system, but your boss has decided that you're the person to create the front end. "And do it in DHTML!" he barks. "Make it look like a software program, not just another Web page!"

◆ Task: Preparing the *Stitch* Page for E-Commerce

In this chapter, we'll simply prepare for creating the page in DHTML. There isn't as much nuts-and-bolts DHTML in this chapter, but it will give you a more complete picture of not only what's possible in DHTML, but also the value of carefully planning a DHTML project. DHTML is so powerful that if you dive into a complicated project without planning it, you'll probably spend most of your time fixing mistakes.

Let's look at how the storefront looks, how we want it to work, and then what DHTML we're going to need to make it work.

◆ Overview of the Storefront

Ideally, we'd like to keep site visitors on the same page until it's absolutely necessary that they go to a different page. This allows for a faster, cleaner user experience since they don't have to wait for a bunch of pages to download.

Since *Stitch* isn't selling many products, we can display them all on the same page along with the Shopping Cart, so visitors don't have to leave the page until they're ready to buy.

The *Stitch* storefront is shown in Figure 4–2.

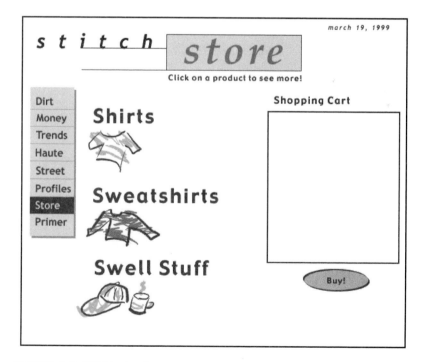

FIGURE 4–2 *Stitch's* storefront

There are two sections of the storefront that site visitors will be concentrating on: the products section and the Shopping Cart. When they first visit this page, their Shopping Cart is empty and they see icons for the three main categories of *Stitch* products: Shirts, Sweatshirts, and Swell Stuff.

Clicking one of those icons causes an animation—the products in the section clicked on glide out horizontally from under the icon, all moving at the same time but at different speeds, so they end up at different places (see Figure 4–3).

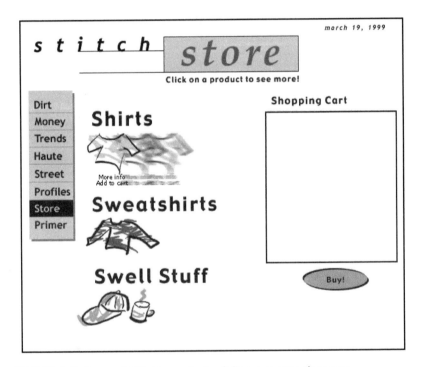

FIGURE 4–3 Some of *Stitch*'s products gliding out onto the page

We'll cover how to animate layers in the next chapter.

If visitors click the "More info" link under the product, a new layer pops up with more information about the product, including available sizes, what material it's made of, and another "Add to cart" link (see Figure 4–4).

Once the products have glided out, visitors can add them to their Shopping Cart in several ways. The first way is by physically

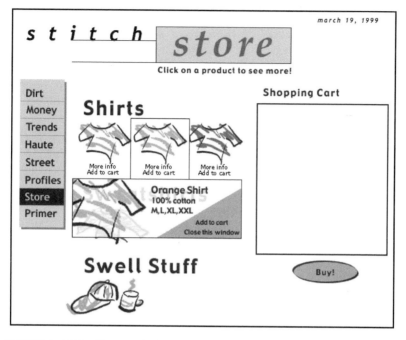

FIGURE 4–4 The "More info" layer made visible

dragging the layer with the product into the Shopping Cart area (we'll cover how to do this in Chapter 6, "Dragging Layers"). The second way to add products to the cart is by clicking the "Add to cart" link underneath each product. The third way is to click the "Add to cart" link in the "More info" layer. Providing many ways to add a product to a Shopping Cart is deliberate—we want to make it as easy as possible for someone to buy something.

When someone adds an item to the Shopping Cart, we'll need to know the quantity and size. So, clicking the "Add to cart" link or dragging the product to the cart area will cause another layer to appear that asks which size and how many of the product the user wants (see Figure 4–5).

Once someone chooses the quantity and size of a certain product he or she wants, we'll display that information in the Shopping Cart. The quantity and size are displayed in form text boxes, while the product name is simply text (see Figure 4–6).

FIGURE 4–5 Making sure we get the site visitor's quantity and size

◆ Setting Up CSS and JavaScript

Now that we know what's going to happen on this page, let's start looking at some of the details. We'll start by creating a backbone of the JavaScript we'll need.

When a visitor clicks a main product icon, we need a function to animate the product rollout.

```
function  animateProductLine ()
{
    1. hide any product line layers currently displayed
       and move those layers back to their original
       position,i.e., underneath the product line icon
    2. animate appropriate product line layers
}
```

If a visitor clicks either of the "Add to cart" links or drags a product to the Shopping Cart, this function gets called:

FIGURE 4–6 The Shopping Cart with a few items

```
function addToCart()
{
    1. hide "more info" box, if visible
    2. pop-up layer asking for quantity and size of product
    3. display appropriate product layer
    4. display quantity in quantity box
    5. display size in size box
}
```

This next function simply displays the "More info" layer:

```
function displayMoreInfo()
{
    hide other more info boxes, if visible
    display appropriate "more info" layer
}
```

The following function deals with dragging the layers. It's complicated and we'll deal with it in Chapter 6.

```
function dragLayer ()
{
```

```
1.     drag and display layer
2.     if layer dragged to basket area:
           addToCart()
       else
           return layer to its original position
   }
```

This final function submits the information in the Shopping Cart to the next page, presumably a page that confirms Shopping Cart contents and gets billing information. The programmers dealing with the back end would tell you how to submit this information, so we'll present this outline here and ignore the details.

```
function goToCheckout()
{
    submit shopping cart information
}
```

Now let's look at the individual layers we'll be using on this page:

We'll want a layer for each of the product line icons and for the blank Shopping Cart (see Figure 4–7).

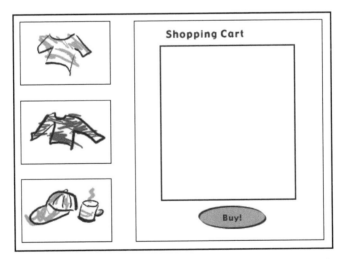

FIGURE 4–7 The three product line layers and the Shopping Cart layer for the *Stitch* Store page

One layer for each product as it rolls out from under the product line icon (see Figure 4–8).

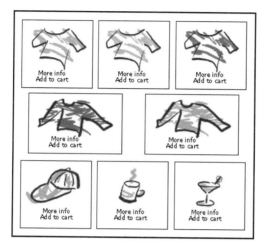

FIGURE 4-8 Each of the *Stitch* products gets its own layer

One layer for each "More info." You'll notice we need transparency in these images so they don't mask the products below them (see Figure 4–9).

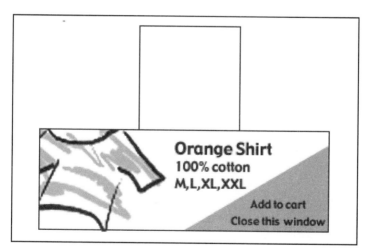

FIGURE 4-9 A "More info" layer. The white inside of the top box is transparent.

One layer asking for the size and quantity of the chosen product (see Figure 4–10).

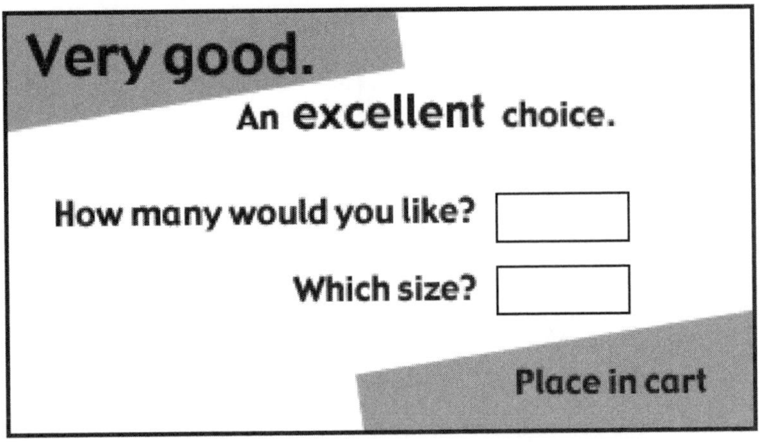

FIGURE 4–10 Before we add anything to the Shopping Cart, we need to know how many and what size

In the Shopping Cart, we need a layer for each product (see Figure 4–11).

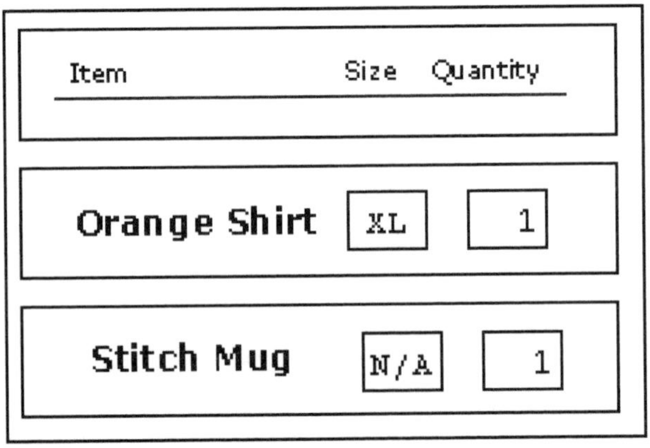

FIGURE 4–11 We need a separate layer for each of these products. Here are two examples.

Other secondary page elements appear as shown in Figure 4–12.

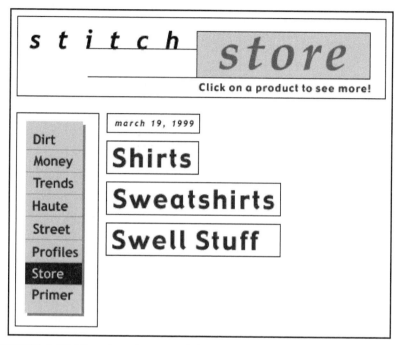

FIGURE 4–12 The other elements of the page

RECAP

We've introduced a much more complicated DHTML project, and showed you some of the more interesting applications of DHTML. You went through a planning process, which is absolutely vital for complex DHTML work. We created a backbone for all the JavaScript and identified all the layers we'll be working with. Doing this type of planning before diving into the project may not be the first thing you want to do, but it'll give you a clearer idea of what's going on and help you avoid backtracking later.

ADVANCED PROJECTS

Create a storefront for a company that's selling 100 products, but let visitors see all the products on the same page.

Also, since the resolution of computer monitors is so low, it'd be nice to show people a larger image of the product if they want to see it. How would you do that?

5 Animating Layers

IN THIS CHAPTER

- Task: Create Animated Product Rollout for Three Product Lines
- Animate a Single Layer
- Animate Multiple Layers
- Another Method
- Recap
- Advanced Projects

◆ Task: Create Animated Product Rollout for Three Product Lines

As described in the preceding chapter, when a visitor clicks one of the three main product icons—Shirts, Sweatshirts, or Swell Stuff—images of the three products in that line glide out horizontally from underneath the main icon, as shown in Figure 5–1.

In this chapter, we'll first look at the code for animating a single layer. Then we'll animate several layers at once and, finally, we'll tweak the code so visitors can look at the animations more than once (which they usually want to do).

FIGURE 5-1 The product layers in motion

WHEN TO ANIMATE

Be judicious in your animation usage. Animations can be useful, but most of the animations currently on the Web are just annoying and distracting. Like all design elements, animations need a reason to be on the page. Before making too many things dance around, ask yourself, "How does this animation enhance the visitor's experience on this page?" and be brutally honest. Remember that most visitors to your site aren't there for your pretty pictures (although they should be, we know), they're there for the content on the page.

◆ Animate a Single Layer

One way to animate a layer is by a series of changes to its specific location. For example, to move the layer shirt1 directly to the coordinates (100,200):

In Netscape:

```
document.layers['shirt1'].left = 100
document.layers['shirt1'].top = 200
```

In Internet Explorer (IE):

```
document.all['shirt1'].style.left = 100
document.all['shirt1'].style.top = 200
```

Using the cross-browser variables we introduced in Chapter 3, "Cross-Browser Coding," we write:

```
eval( layerRef + "['shirt1']" + styleRef +
".left  = 100")
eval( layerRef + "['shirt1']" + styleRef +
".top  = 200")
```

POSITIONING

All coordinates are measured from the upper-left corner of the browser window.

When you position a layer at coordinates (x,y), that's where the upper-left corner of the layer will be positioned.

For this animation, we'll create a loop that increments the left coordinate and then moves the image to that coordinate. Say we have a layer called shirt1 that we want to animate from its starting position at a left coordinate of 100 pixels. We want to move it 100 pixels to the right, one pixel at a time. We'll call this function with the following link:

```
<A HREF="javascript: moveShirt(100)">move the shirt</A>
```

And here's the function:

```
function moveShirt(shirt1Position)
{
```
1.
```
    if (shirt1Position < 201)
    {
        shirt1Position ++
    }
    else
    {
```
2.
```
        // breaks the loop
        return
    }
```
3.
```
    // change the layer's position
    eval ( layerRef + "['shirt1']" + styleRef +
    ".left = " + shirt1Position )
```
4.
```
    // pause briefly, then run this function again
    setTimeout('moveShirt(' + shirt1Position + ')', 1)
}
```

HOW THE CODE WORKS

1. First, we're setting the limit at 201, because we don't want the layer to go further than that.

2. When it does hit 201, `return` stops the function in its tracks.

3. Let's look at this without the `eval()`, because it's easier to read that way. In Netscape, this line would look like:

   ```
   document.layers['shirt1'].left = shirt1Position
   ```

   In IE, it'd look like:

   ```
   document.all['shirt1'].style.left = 100
   ```

4. Now that we've moved the layer over one pixel, we're going to repeat the process by calling the function again. First, however, we have to pause briefly to give the browser time to actually draw the layer in its new position—that's what the `setTimeout` is for, even though it's set to pause only for a hundredth of a second. If you run this code without the `setTimeout`, the code happens so fast that the animation doesn't occur. The browser simply pauses, and the last "frame" of the animation appears—the layer simply jumps 100 pixels to the right.

   One advantage to this method is that the site visitor can run the animation multiple times by clicking the link; you don't need a special function to reset the layer's position. This is possible because information in the link `<A HREF="javascript: moveShirt(100)">` tells the JavaScript to position the layer at whatever coordinate is passed to the function; in this case, 100.

◆ Animate Multiple Layers

In this case, animating multiple layers is also relatively simple. Of course, the more complicated your motion, the more complicated the code will be. If you want the layers to move in figure 8s instead of straight lines, you'll have some serious math to work through.

In this case, we want the three layers to start in the same position and move in the same direction, but glide out at different speeds, so they end up at different locations along a straight line. The changes to the code are relatively minor.

```
function moveShirt(shirt1Position, shirt2Position,
                   shirt3Position)
{
    if (shirt1Position < 201)
    {
        // change the position of the layers
        shirt1Position ++
        shirt2Position = shirt2Position + 2
        shirt3Position = shirt3Position + 3
    }
    else
    {
        // breaks the loop
        return
    }

    // change the layers' position
    eval ( layerRef + "['shirt1']" + styleRef +
    ".left = " + shirt1Position )
    eval ( layerRef + "['shirt2']" + styleRef +
    ".left = " + shirt2Position )
    eval ( layerRef + "['shirt3']" + styleRef +
    ".left = " + shirt3Position )

    // pause briefly, then do it again
    setTimeout('moveShirt(' + shirt1Position + ',' +
    shirt2Position + ',' + shirt3Position + ')', 1)
}
```

1. (marginal note, pointing at the `// change the position of the layers` block)

HOW THE CODE WORKS

1. We're changing the position of the layers at different rates. Shirt 1 creeps along a pixel at a time, while Shirt 2 jumps two pixels, and Shirt 3 leaps three pixels at a time.

POSITIONING LAYERS OFF-SCREEN

You can place images partially or completely off-screen by using negative coordinates. For example:

```
document.layers['shirt1'].left = -100
```

will work fine. This is a good way to position layers if you want to fly them off the screen. You can also use:

```
#shirt1
{
    position: absolute;
    top: -100px;
    left: -100px;
}
```

to initially place an image off-screen and then move it on-screen later. Sometimes, doing this will cause a browser to show scroll bars, even if the user can't scroll.

◆ Another Method

Sometimes, you'll want to animate a layer when you don't know what its position is. Maybe you've enabled dragging the layer, which we'll discuss in Chapter 6, or there's been a series of animations and it'd be difficult to keep track of where everything was, or maybe you're animating 20 small layers at once. You can move layers by nudging them over a few pixels instead of determining their absolute position, but of course, Netscape and IE have completely different syntax for this.

If you want your layer to move three pixels to the left and seven pixels down:

In Netscape:

```
document.layers['shirt1'].moveBy (3,7)
```

In IE:

```
document.all.['shirt1'].style.pixelLeft = 3
document.all.['shirt1'].style.pixelTop = 7
```

Unfortunately, the syntax of these two methods are so different that you can't use the eval() statement without creating totally unreadable code. A better solution is to determine which browser is being used as soon as the page is loaded.

```
<SCRIPT LANGUAGE="JavaScript">
// Global variables for platform branching
var isNav, isIE
if (parseInt(navigator.appVersion) >= 4)
{
    if (navigator.appName == "Netscape")
```

```
    {
        isNav = true
    }
    else
    {
        isIE = true
    }
}
```

This way, when we come up against some commands that have completely different syntax in Netscape and IE, we can do this:

```
if (isNav)
{
    // Netscape commands
}
else
{
    // IE commands
}
```

The code that actually moves the layers around looks like this:

```
if (isNav)
{
    document.layers['shirt1'].moveBy(3,7)
}
else
{
    document.all.['shirt1'].style.pixelLeft = 3
    document.all.['shirt1'].style.pixelTop = 7
}
```

It's clunky and a pain to go through an `if` statement every time you want to do an animation, but we recommend either doing it this way or by using absolute coordinates discussed earlier.

RECAP

You now know the basics of animating layers in DHTML. We can animate single or multiple layers by changing the layer's absolute coordinates using the `.left` and `.top` attributes in layers in JavaScript. With a little more coding we can animate layers by telling JavaScript to move a layer by a certain amount of pixels instead of by absolute coordinates.

ADVANCED PROJECTS

You can tell we're just scratching the surface of what's possible for animating layers. As an exercise, write a function that will move the three shirt icons in from off-screen at a 45° angle. And, if you're feeling spunky, change the speed of the individual shirts; that is, have them start moving fast and then slow down as they reach their destination. Hint: Use another variable to determine how far they move:

```
shirt1Position = shirt1Position + step
```

chapter

6 Dragging Layers

In This Chapter

- Task: Create Draggable Layers for Placing Products in the Shopping Cart
- How the Code Works
- The Meat of the Code
- What We Left Out
- Recap
- Advanced Projects

◆ Task: Create Draggable Layers for Placing Products in the Shopping Cart

To introduce a new level of interactivity to the *Stitch* Store page, we're going to let people add products to their shopping cart by actually dragging the image of the product to a section of the page called "Shopping Cart."

Once the image is dragged to the cart area, a window will appear asking for the quantity and size of the item the user wants. Once those questions are answered, the image of the product will return to its original position and a text layer will appear in the Shopping Cart describing the product selection the user just made (see Figures 6–1 through 6–3).

FIGURE 6–1 User dragging an image to the Shopping Cart

◆ How the Code Works

The code to drag layers is more complicated than anything we've seen yet, and we'll introduce more new commands, functions, and ideas here than in the earlier chapters. You'll be learning a lot of new stuff in this chapter, so make yourself some tea, find a quiet room, and hunker down.

Events

The biggest new thing to learn is something called *events*. Events are things the user does, like clicking the mouse or typing on the keyboard. There's a little more to it than that, however. Clicking your mouse causes an event, and it also sends information as to where the cursor was when you clicked the mouse. When you use a word processor, the program needs to know where to place the text you're typing in. So, events are actions the user takes along with information about where the cursor is when the event occurs.

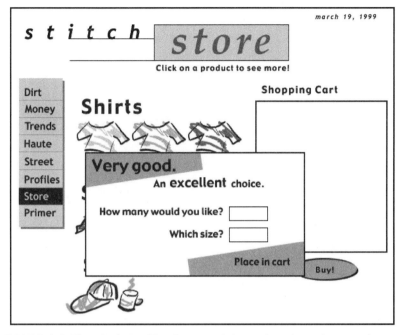

FIGURE 6–2 The window asking for more information about the quantity and sizes wanted

When we want to drag a layer, we need to tell the browser to look for certain events, like clicking, dragging the mouse, and releasing the mouse button. Then we need to tell the browser to execute certain commands when those events happen.

In Netscape, the command to set the browser on edge to constantly look for certain events is

```
document.captureEvents(Event.MOUSEDOWN | Event.MOUSEMOVE
| Event.MOUSEUP)
```

This causes the browser to look for the user pushing the mouse button down, moving the mouse (whether the button is down or not), and releasing the mouse button. This command isn't necessary in Internet Explorer (IE).

We'll then tell the browser to execute certain commands when those events are detected. If we have three main functions that do something when the user clicks the mouse button, moves the mouse, or releases the mouse button, the code will look like this:

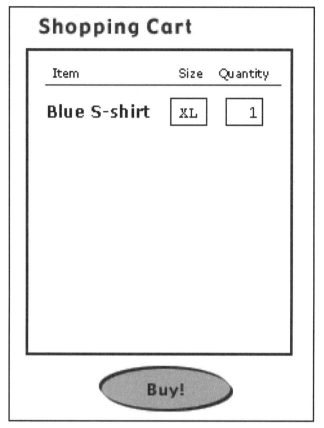

FIGURE 6–3 The item now appears in the Shopping Cart

```
document.onmousedown = grabProduct
document.onmousemove = dragProduct
document.onmouseup = releaseProduct
```

The three functions are `grabProduct`, `dragProduct`, and `releaseProduct`. Don't worry that the parentheses that usually show up after a function name, for example, `checkForm()`, aren't in this section of code. You don't need them in this case.

Other common events that aren't listed here are `onmouseover` and `onmouseout`.

Before going further, we'd like to thank Danny Goodman of Netscape for coming up with the basic structure of the code in this chapter. He's a damn fine programmer. If you meet him in a bar, buy him a drink.

Browser Differences

Unfortunately, Netscape and IE harbor significant differences when it comes to dealing with events and positioning layers, much like we saw at the end of the preceding chapter. These differences are so extreme that the usual cross-browser coding tricks we showed you in Chapter 3 result in amazingly complicated and unreadable code. We're going to repeat the better code snippet here:

```
<SCRIPT LANGUAGE="JavaScript">
// Global variables for browser determination
var isNav, isIE
if (parseInt(navigator.appVersion) >= 4)
{
    if (navigator.appName == "Netscape")
    {
        isNav = true
    }
    else
    {
        isIE = true
    }
}
```

This way, when we come up against some commands that have completely different syntax in Netscape and IE, we can do this:

```
if (isNav)
{
    // Netscape commands would go here
}
else
{
    // IE commands would go here
}
```

Objects

We'll be using something called *objects* in this code as well. You've heard of object-oriented programming—here's a little taste of it. The objects we'll be using are pretty simple and will look a lot like a variable. For example:

```
testObject = document.layers[4]
```

is a valid object: We take whatever is on layer 4 and call it `test-Object`. The advantage to this is that you can then manipulate that object/layer by using just the object name. For example, to move that object 100 pixels to the right and 150 pixels down, use this code:

```
if (isNav)
{
    testObject.moveBy(100,150)
}
else
{
    testObject.pixelLeft = 100
    testObject.pixelTop = 150
}
```

Like events, the full story about objects is much more complicated, and they're more powerful than we're showing here. However, you don't need to know more in order to make this code work just fine.

Dragging and User Interface

Just writing code to drag an image isn't enough. We want the dragging to mimic what people are used to: dragging icons and windows across their desktop. When you drag these items, they're placed on top of all other elements on the screen (with very few exceptions), and when the items are dragged, they maintain the same spatial relationship with the cursor as when the cursor first clicked on the item. That's what people are accustomed to, and that's what they'll expect to see. So let's look at what we need to do to accomplish this.

DRAGGING ON TOP

When we drag a product image, we'd like it to be above all the other layers. Otherwise, we'll be dragging a layer underneath other layers, and that's bad user interface. To make sure that the layer is on top while we're dragging it, we need to temporarily change its z-index while it's being dragged. We'll go a little overboard and move the layers to a z-index of 100 when they're being dragged. Here's how to do that:

```
function setZIndex(obj, objZindex)
{
    obj.zIndex = objZindex
}
```

So, when the object starts to get dragged, we'll call this function with:

```
setZIndex (draggedObj, 100)
```

When the user stops dragging the layer, we'll want to set it back to its original z-index, so we'll call this function again, but with a different value for the z-index:

```
setZIndex (draggedObj, 1)
```

KEEPING THE CURSOR IN THE RIGHT PLACE

Another user interface issue to deal with is where the user clicks inside the image and how he or she drags it. We want the image to stay in the same place relative to where the user clicks on it. That is, if the user clicks on the right side of the image and drags, we want the cursor to stay on the right side of the image as it moves. This may seem obvious, but it requires some special coding to achieve. Otherwise, wherever the user clicked in the image, the image would immediately move so that the upper left-hand corner would be under the cursor.

To deal with this, we need to look at where the user actually clicked on the layer and measure how far that click occurred from the edge of the layer. Then, when the user starts to drag the layer, we can use that measurement to make sure the layer's position stays relative to the cursor position.

Where the user clicks on the page is called the *event coordinate*. Once again, Netscape and IE deal with this in different ways, as shown in the following code:

```
     if (isNav)
     {
1.      offsetX = evt.pageX - selectedProduct.left
        offsetY = evt.pageY - selectedProduct.top
     }
     else
     {
2.      offsetX = window.event.offsetX
        offsetY = window.event.offsetY
     }
```

where `selectedProduct` is the *Stitch* product the user has clicked on.

HOW THE CODE WORKS

1. `evt.pageX` and `evt.pageY` are the event coordinates. If a user clicks on the screen in Netscape, you can find out where that click occurred with `evt.pageX` and `evt.pageY`. As you've probably guessed, `clickX` gives us the value of the x-coordinate of where the event occurred on the page, and `clickY` gives us the value of the y-coordinate of where the event occurred. And as mentioned previously, `selected-Product` is the *Stitch* product the user has clicked on; it's assumed that we've already determined which product that is and have created an object called `selectedProduct`.

2. In this case, IE looks at where the click occurred, looks at the top layer underneath that click, and assumes that's the layer you're interested in. The offset between where the user clicked and the edge of the layer is automatically calculated by `window.event.offsetX` and `window.event.offsetY`.

Clipping Regions

For coding the Netscape section of this code, we'll need to learn a new property: clipping regions. A layer's clipping region is the size of the displayed area. For example, if a layer contains a simple image 300 pixels wide, the clipping width of that layer is 300. To find a layer's clipping width and height:

```
x = document.layers[4].clip.width
y = document.layers[4].clip.height
```

Since we're going to be referring to layers using objects, our reference to layers will look more like:

```
selectedProduct = document.layers[4]
```

Thus, our code using clipping will look more like this:

```
x = selectedProduct.clip.width
```

Clipping height and width is also something you can set, if you want to only show part of an image. Changing the clipping region doesn't affect the layer at all, it just changes how much of the layer is displayed. We won't be changing the clipping area in this example, but if you wanted to display only the right half of a 400 x 300 pixel image, the code would look like:

```
#layerToBeClipped
{
    position: absolute;
    top: 50px;
    left: 100px;
    clip: rect(0px 400px 200px 300px)
}
```

The format for setting a clipping region is

```
clip: rect(top right bottom left)
```

◆ The Meat of the Code

Now you're ready for the juicy stuff. We've shown you some important pieces of the code and some of the new concepts and properties
we'll be using. The following code works great for dragging layers,
but we've left out some customization that will have to be included
in the *Stitch* page. We did this to keep the code simple, but we'll add
the customized parts later in this chapter. For now, concentrate on
the basic dragging code, and then we'll add to it later.

Here's the code:

```
<SCRIPT LANGUAGE="JavaScript">
```
1.
```
// Global variables for platform branching
var isNav, isIE
if (parseInt(navigator.appVersion) >= 4)
{
    if (navigator.appName == "Netscape")
    {
        isNav = true
    }
    else
    {
        isIE = true
    }
}
```

2.
```
// ***Begin Utility Functions***
```

3.
```
// Set zIndex property
function setzIndex(product, zOrder)
{
    product.zIndex = zOrder
}
```

4.
```
// Position an object at a specific pixel coordinate
function shiftTo(product, x, y)
{
    if (isNav)
    {
        product.moveTo(x,y)
    }
    else
    {
        product.pixelLeft = x
        product.pixelTop = y
    }
}

// ***End Utility Functions***
```

5.
```
// Global variable that holds reference to selected
element var selectedProduct
```

6.
```
// Global variables that hold location of click relative
to element var offsetX, offsetY
```

7.
```
// Find out which element has been clicked on
function setSelectedElem(evt)
{
    if (isNav)
    {
```
8.
```
        var clickX = evt.pageX
        var clickY = evt.pageY
        var testObj
```
9.
```
        for (var i = document.layers.length - 1; i >= 0; i--)
        {
```
10.
```
            testObj = document.layers[i]
```
11.
```
            if ((clickX > testObj.left) &&
                (clickX < testObj.left + testObj.clip.width)
                && (clickY > testObj.top) &&
                (clickY < testObj.top + testObj.clip.height))
            {
```
12.
```
                selectedProduct = testObj
```
13.
```
                if (selectedProduct)
                {
                    setZIndex(selectedProduct, 100)
                    return
                }
            }
        }
    }
    else
    {
```

```
14.        var imgObj = window.event.srcElement
15.        selectedProduct = imgObj.parentElement.style
16.        if (selectedProduct)
           {
               setzIndex(selectedProduct,100)
               return
           }
       }

17.    selectedProduct = null
       return
   }

18. // Drag an element
   function dragProduct(evt)
   {
19.    if (selectedProduct)
       {
           if (isNav)
           {
20.            shiftTo(selectedProduct, (evt.pageX - offsetX),
                       (evt.pageY - offsetY))
           }
           else
           {
21.            shiftTo(selectedProduct,
                       (window.event.clientX - offsetX),
                       (window.event.clientY - offsetY))
22.            // prevent further system response to dragging
               return false
           }
       }
   }

23. // Turn selected element on
   function grabProduct(evt)
   {
24.    setSelectedElem(evt)
25.    if (selectedProduct)
       {
26.        if (isNav)
           {
               offsetX = evt.pageX - selectedProduct.left
               offsetY = evt.pageY - selectedProduct.top
           }
           else
           {
27.            offsetX = window.event.offsetX
               offsetY = window.event.offsetY
```

```
            }
        }

        // prevent further processing of mouseDown event so
        // that the Macintosh doesn't display the contextual
        // menu and lets dragging work normally.

        return false
    }
```

28.
```
    // Turn selected element off
    function releaseProduct(evt)
    {
```
29.
```
        setzIndex(selectedProduct, 0)
        selectedProduct = null
    }
```

30.
```
    // Set event capture for Navigator
    function setNSEventCapture()
    {
        if (isNav)
        {
            document.captureEvents(Event.MOUSEDOWN |
            Event.MOUSEMOVE | Event.MOUSEUP)
        }
    }
```

31.
```
    // Assign event handlers used by both Navigator and IE
    function init()
    {
```
32.
```
        if (isNav)
        {
            setNSEventCapture()
        }
```
33.
```
        document.onmousedown = grabProduct
        document.onmousemove = dragProduct
        document.onmouseup = releaseProduct
    }
    </SCRIPT>

    <BODY onLoad="init()">
```

HOW THE CODE WORKS

Ready? We recommend you stretch a little now.

1. The first thing we do is determine which browser is being used to view the page. We'll use this information a lot, since Netscape and IE use significantly different syntax to capture events and position layers.

2. We're creating a set of Utility Functions. These are sets of commands that are used frequently by other functions. By separating these frequently used commands, we don't have to code them several times within other functions.

3. The first Utility Function is the setting of the z-index, which happens twice. The first time we set a z-index is when a user clicks on a draggable image—since we want to drag that layer over the top of the other layers, we'll increase the z-index while it's being dragged. The second time we'll change the z-index is when the user stops dragging the layer. When that happens, we'll drop the layer back to its original z-index.

4. The next Utility Function moves a layer to a specified position. Since Netscape and IE use different syntax to achieve this, we split the function into two pieces. We could have coded these commands into another function, but the code is much more readable (and easier to debug) when these commands are pulled into a separate function.

5. When a user clicks on a product, we need a way to remember which layer they clicked on and a way to refer to that layer. We do this with the global variable selected-Product. It starts out as a variable, but we make it an object once we have a layer to assign to it.

6. We also need to keep track of the relative position of where the user clicked in the layer to the edge of the layer. We keep track of that pixel offset with the variables offsetX and offsetY.

7. This function is probably the most complicated of the whole script. When the user clicks on the page, it's vital that we figure out which layer he or she actually clicked on. As you'll see, this is more difficult to do in Netscape than in IE.

8. The first two variables, clickX and clickY, find out where on the page the user clicked using the evt.pageX and evt.pageY event coordinates. The next variable, testObj, is a layer placeholder: While we cycle through all the layers to see which one the user clicked on, we'll keep track of which layer we're looking at using testObj. Again, this starts out as a variable, but we make it an object by assigning it to a layer.

9. To look at all the layers, we're going to start at the top layer and work our way down. We find out how many layers exist through `document.layers.length` and then set up a `for` loop to cycle through them all.

10. We set `testObj` to be the layer we're currently looking at.

11. This massive `if` statement looks to see if the user click occurred within the displayed part of the layer. `testObj.left` is the distance from the left edge of the browser window to the left edge of the layer in question. (`testObj.left + testObj.clip.width`) is the pixel coordinate of the right edge of the viewable part of the layer. It's the left edge coordinate (`testObj.left`) plus the width of the viewable area (`testObj.clip.width`).

12. We cement `selectedProduct` to whichever layer we're looking at via `testObj`.

13. This `if` statement makes sure that we're dealing with a layer that actually exists. It acts as an extra confirmation. If the layer does exist, that means the user clicked on it, so we set the stage for dragging by setting the z-index to 100, which decisively places the layer above all the others. We then `return`, which stops the function in its tracks and returns it to whatever function called it (we'll see the function that called this one layer in the code).

14. We now engage in the IE method of selecting the appropriate layer. This is much easier: To find out which element was clicked on we only need to call `window.event .srcElement`, which gives us the element that was the source of the event (in this case, the user clicking the mouse).

15. `imgObj.parentElement.style` gives us the actual layer.

16. We now do what we did in item #13: We make sure that `selectedProduct` exists, and then prepare it for dragging by bumping up its z-index to 100.

17. If no layer was clicked on, (for example, the user clicked on some whitespace), we make `selectedProduct` null, which is the same as saying that no product is selected.

18. This is a function that actually moves the selected layer around. It's called by the event handler line `document .onmousemove = dragProduct`, which we'll look at in

detail later. When the user moves the mouse (whether he or she is dragging or not), the `dragProduct` function is called.

19. Since `dragProduct` is called whether or not the user is dragging, we have to make sure that the user is actually dragging something before we start moving layers around. We do that by checking to see if `selectedProduct` exists. If it does, that means the user is dragging a layer and we want to move the layer around. If `selectedProduct` doesn't exist, that means the user is just moving the mouse around and we don't want to move any layers around.

20. After we determine that the user is dragging a product (and is using Netscape), we move the layer to the event coordinates where the user dragged the mouse (`evt.pageX` and `evt.pageY`) offset by the relative position of the cursor to the edge of the layer (`offsetX` and `offsetY`).

21. The code for IE is similar. The only difference is how to refer to where the user clicked on the page. Instead of Netscape's `evt.pageX` and `evt.pageY`, IE uses `window.event.clientX` and `window.event.clientY`. Otherwise, it's the same code.

22. We then `return false` so that the script doesn't keep moving the layers on its own, but requires the user to keep moving the mouse.

23. The function `grabProduct` is called by the event `handler` `document.onmousedown = grabProduct`, so any time the user clicks the mouse button, `grabProduct` leaps into action. This function determines which layer was clicked on and what the cursor offset is.

24. The layer that was clicked on is determined by the `setSelectedElem(evt)` function, which we looked at in detail earlier. You have to pass the `(evt)` to `setSelectedElem` so the function has the information it needs in order to figure out which layer was clicked on.

25. We then make sure that a layer was actually clicked on before we proceed to figure out the cursor offset.

26. In order to determine the cursor offset in Netscape, we have to use `evt.pageX` and `evt.pageY` with the edges of the layer the user clicked on, `selectedProduct`.

27. Determining the offset is much easier in IE because it calculates it automatically for you with `window.event .offsetX` and `window.event.offsetY`.

28. When the user releases the mouse button (handled by `document.onmouseup = releaseProduct`), the `release-Product` function is called. The purpose of this function is simply to set everything back to normal, back to the state before the user clicked on anything.

29. The `selectedProduct` gets its z-index set back to zero, where it started. `selectedProduct` also gets wiped clean in preparation for the next time the user clicks the mouse button.

30. Although this code occurs late in the script, it's one of the first things that happens. If you want Netscape to look for user events and capture them, you have to tell it explicitly what to look for using the `document.captureEvents()` statement. Any number of events can be looked for, not just the three we're after: MOUSEDOWN, MOUSEMOVE, and MOUSEUP. A list of all events is in Appendix B, "Miscellaneous Reference."

31. The `init()` function is the function called as soon as the page is loaded, so its commands get executed immediately, without the user doing anything. The purpose of this function is to start looking for user events and set what functions get called once those functions occur; in other words, event capture and handling. We call this function as soon as the page is loaded because we want the browser to start looking for events immediately.

32. As we mentioned earlier, Netscape needs a special command to start looking for events.

33. This is the event handling part of the code. It tells the browser which function to go to when certain events happen. That is, if a user clicks the mouse button, execute `grabProduct`. If the user moves the mouse, execute `dragProduct`. If the user lets go of the mouse button, execute `releaseProduct`. Note that Windows users clicking the right mouse button won't cause the `grabProduct` function to be called—only the left button does that.

◆ What We Left Out

As complicated and involved as this code is, we left out a number of features that are required to make this page work the way we want it to. Here's a list of what remains:

1. As the code stands, every single layer on the page is draggable. We only want the product layers to be draggable, and we only want them to be draggable when the animation has occurred and they're displayed side by side, as shown in Figure 6–4.

2. The code now leaves images wherever the user dragged them. For the *Stitch* page, if the products are dragged to the Shopping Cart, we want the product image to snap back to its original position and have a layer appear that asks for product size and quantity. If the product is dragged somewhere else besides the Shopping Cart, we just want to snap it back to its original position with no further action.

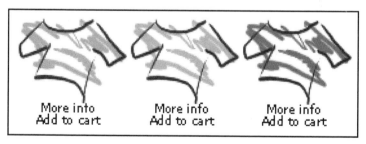

FIGURE 6–4 The products hidden under the product line icon and fully displayed

Because the real goal of this chapter is to show you how to drag layers and not build every nuance of the *Stitch* page, we'll leave these two items unfinished.

RECAP

We covered a lot—a whole lot. In the process of learning how to drag layers, you've seen:

- Event capturing
- Event handling
- Using objects
- Clipping regions
- Another method of dealing with both browsers
- Functions calling other functions
- How to solve some user interface issues

Congratulations on getting through this chapter. It's certainly the most involved so far. In the next chapter, we'll use all of the concepts presented so far in this book and apply them to a very interactive page for Shelley Biotech.

ADVANCED PROJECTS

See that list under "What We Left Out?" Start by coding to solve #2—it's easier. Then, if you feel lucky, start in on #1, but expect to spend a lot of time on it. It'll take some work, but your understanding of how DHTML works will advance significantly.

7 A Really Interactive Quiz: Part One

In This Chapter

- Task: Create a Fully Interactive Quiz for Shelley Biotechnologies
- The Functional Spec
- Building the Questions
- Cycling through the Questions
- Recap
- Advanced Projects

◆ Task: Create a Fully Interactive Quiz for Shelley Biotechnologies

Shelley Biotechnologies creates some pretty complicated products for difficult-to-learn purposes. The company caters to people who already know a lot about biotechnology, but the more people who know about biotech, the more people Shelley can cater to. With that in mind, Shelley decided to create a quiz about one of its more obtuse products, the Quantum-Chaos rDNA Compiler. This machine uses quantum computing (using individual atoms to store information as 0s and 1s—which is real technology, by the way), a branch of mathematics known as Chaos to filter out some noise in the data that occurs as a result of using quantum mechanics. Based on these technologies, this machine creates strands of rDNA, which are little strings of genetic code that are copied from master DNA strands and then used as templates to create proteins and enzymes. It's hard-core stuff and Shelley needs all the help it can get to market these things to the man and woman on the street. Therefore, the marketing folks at Shelley have come to you, in all your DHTML wisdom, to create a wildly interactive quiz for them with moving layers and draggable layers and all sorts of stuff.

This quiz will use most of what we've learned in this book, so most of it will be implementing techniques you are already familiar with (although in different ways), but you'll be learning some brand new stuff along the way, too.

◆ The Functional Spec

A project with as many different parts as a fully interactive quiz requires some forethought before you just jump into coding. Once we've figured out the vision, making a lot of the individual decisions becomes easier.

The overall goal of the quiz is to increase Shelley Biotech's bottom line; if you can't figure out how a part of a Web site increases a company's revenue, it should probably be cut. The quiz will indirectly increase Shelley's financials through several avenues: educating users about Shelley's products, gaining mindshare by keeping those users on the site while they take the quiz (and are looking at Shelley's name and logo for the whole time), and by, hopefully, creating a minor buzz about the cool quiz so more users will visit the site, further increasing mindshare and knowledge about Shelley and its products. As a programmer, this marketing stuff may not be the most interesting part to you, but it's absolutely vital to the life of the Web site.

The secondary goals are to educate the user about Shelley's products and have the quiz be entertaining enough that the user completes the quiz and tells others about it. The user must actually learn something about the product while enjoying the experience enough to stay and tell others.

Educating the user about the product isn't really your job, it's the job of the people who write the quiz. Making the experience enjoyable and interactive is your job. And since you're a DHTML whiz and thus good at user interfaces, you're perfect for this task.

Remember, you're not building a simple Web page here, you're writing a small software application. Before tackling any project of this size, you need to spell out to yourself what's going to happen in this quiz, what all the pieces are, what they do, and where they'll be on the page.

The Quiz Questions

So here's the scoop. The quiz will have 10 questions, and they'll be worth 10 points each. Each question will live on its own layer. Most questions will be multiple choice, so most questions will have several radio buttons, and all the questions will have two buttons at the bottom: "Answer" to submit the question for scoring, and "Skip" to pass on the current question and go to the next one.

Some of the questions will have animations and a couple will have draggable layers in them. From a coding perspective, this means that we're going to have nested layers: A question layer may have a few sublayers inside of it, and we're going to animate or drag those sublayers without touching the question layer as a whole.

Scoring

After the user answers each question by pressing the "Answer" button, the code will see whether the user chose the right answer or not and will display a layer with the appropriate message. However, for a few questions, if the user chooses a wrong answer that is very close to the right answer, a layer will appear giving the user a choice: he or she can get a hint, and guess again for partial credit of five points. However, if the user guesses wrong again after getting the hint, he or she will lose five points.

The user's ongoing score will be displayed in a text box on the right side of the screen. This score will be updated every time a question is answered. Along with a simple numerical score will be a sentence with an ongoing evaluation like "You're doing really well," or "You're starting to choke," or "You're a genius. You should work for us."

Progress/Navigation

Underneath the ongoing score updates will be a series of small page icons that will track the user's progress through the quiz. Each question gets a little icon, and the icon will be grayed out when the user answers that question. This lets the user know how much of the quiz he or she has completed and how much further there is to go. If the user skips a question, that question's icon doesn't get grayed out, and the user can click on that icon to go back and answer the question (see Figure 7–1).

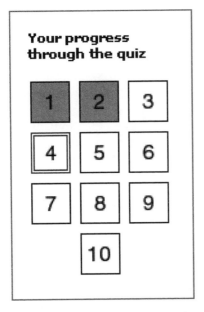

FIGURE 7–1 The User Progress section of the quiz, with completed questions in gray, incomplete questions in white, and the current question with a black border

After the Quiz

When the quiz is completed, a layer appears that congratulates the user and gives the overall score. The user is also presented with some links that go to several sections of the Shelley site that deal with the functions of the Quantum-Chaos rDNA Compiler, as well as a "Time to brag and gloat! E-mail your score to a friend!" link that acts as another marketing tool to spread the word about the quiz.

◆ Building the Questions

We want the questions to look something like Figure 7–2.

Where we place the image(s) used and the multiple choices will vary some from question to question, but we want to keep the text styles in each question the same. The only variation we want is to have different colors for the text of each question. It'll be a subtle difference using dark colors, but we want each one to be different. This creates an interesting style problem.

Question #2

What percentage of the rDNA strands harvested by the Quantum-Chaos rDNA Compiler are unbroken?

 100%

○ 50%

○ 99%

[Skip] [Answer]

FIGURE 7–2 A sample question

We want the headline of each question (for example, "Question #5") to be 16 points and bold in a sans-serif font, preferably Verdana. If Verdana is not available on the user's system, then we want to use the system's default sans-serif font (Arial on Windows and Helvetica on Macs). We want the body of the question to be in regular Times at 12 point, and the question's choices to be 12-point Times, but bold.

Here's how we set it up:

1.
```
#question1
{
    position: absolute;
    top: 100px;
    left: 100px;
    visibility: visible;
    color: purple;
}

#question2
{
    position: absolute;
    top: 100px;
    left: 100px;
    visibility: hidden;
    color: darkred;
}
```

2.  ```
    .questionHeader
    {
        font-size: 16pt;
        font-family: verdana, sans-serif;
        font-weight: bold;
    }
    .questionChoices { font-weight: bold; font-size: 12pt }
    .questionText { font-size: 12pt }
    ```

HOW THE CODE WORKS

1. We're placing each question in its own layer so they're easier to deal with as whole units. Notice we're also setting the color for each question here and not in a class somewhere else.

2. We're creating three classes to deal with the text differences among all of the questions.

Here's the HTML for the first question:

```
<DIV ID="question1">
  <SPAN CLASS="questionHeader">Question #1</SPAN>
  <P>
  <SPAN CLASS="questionText">
        Will the Quantum-Chaos rDNA Compiler also create
the actual proteins that would be encoded from the rDNA
strands?
  <FORM NAME="question1Form">
    <TABLE>
      <TR>
        <TD>
          <INPUT TYPE="radio" NAME="question1Options">
        </TD>
        <TD>
          <SPAN CLASS="questionChoices">Yes</SPAN>
        </TD>
      </TR>
      <TR>
        <TD>
          <INPUT TYPE="radio" NAME="question1Options">
        </TD>
        <TD>
          <SPAN CLASS="questionChoices">No</SPAN>
        </TD>
      </TR>
    </TABLE>
    <P>
```
```

```
<INPUT TYPE="button" VALUE="Skip" NAME="skip"
onClick="skipQuestion(1)">
<INPUT TYPE="button" VALUE="Answer" NAME="answer"
onClick="checkAnswer(1)">
</FORM>
</SPAN>
</DIV>
```

We're using a table in the form to make sure the radio buttons and the text next to them stay nicely aligned. Let's see what that looks like in both browsers (see Figures 7–3 and 7–4).

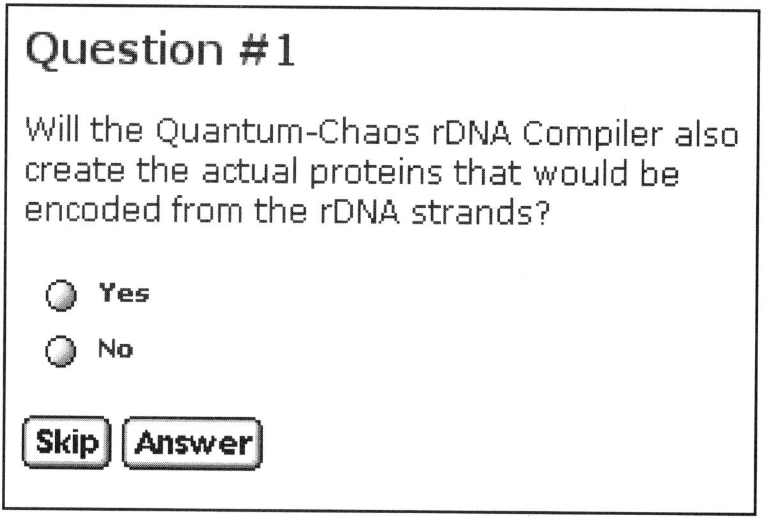

Question #1

Will the Quantum-Chaos rDNA Compiler also create the actual proteins that would be encoded from the rDNA strands?

○ Yes

○ No

[Skip] [Answer]

FIGURE 7–3 Question #1 in Internet Explorer 4

Uh oh. The font family and blue color disappeared in the question choices in Netscape. The <SPAN> for the question options worked fine—the words are bold and 12 point—but the earlier classes that should be inherited are stopped cold by the <TABLE> in Netscape. As soon as you mix DHTML and tables in Netscape, chances are things won't work as you expect and you'll have to create workarounds. Accept it now and save heartache later.

The workaround here is unfortunate, but it works. Add several color classes to your stylesheet and use those classes on the individual question choices.

```
.purple {color: purple}
```

Question #1

Will the Quantum-Chaos rDNA Compiler also create the actual proteins that would be encoded from the rDNA strands?

 Yes

 No

FIGURE 7–4 Question #1 in Netscape Navigator 4

and in the `<BODY>`

```
<TABLE>
   <TR>
     <TD>
       <INPUT TYPE="radio" NAME="question1Options">
     </TD>
     <TD>
       <SPAN CLASS="questionChoices">
       <SPAN CLASS="purple">
       Yes
       </SPAN>
       </SPAN>
     </TD>
   </TR>
   <TR>
     <TD>
       <INPUT TYPE="radio" NAME="question1Options">
     </TD>
     <TD>
       <SPAN CLASS="questionChoices">
       <SPAN CLASS="purple">
       No
       </SPAN>
       </SPAN>
     </TD>
```

```
</TR>
</TABLE>
```

Yes, this muddies up your code and adds some extra work. There are a few other workarounds, but they're not any prettier.

THE WEB STANDARDS PROJECT

No Web designer or programmer likes these differences between the browsers. Both Netscape and Microsoft will ballyhoo their dedication to standards and claim that their browser is more standard-compliant than the other. In all fairness, they're both making strides in the next generation of browsers.

Not satisfied with simply making strides, a group of Web designers, programmers, and architects has been created to demand that Netscape and Microsoft create browsers that completely conform to standards set forth by the World Wide Web Consortium, the group that tells us what's a standard and what isn't. The rapidly growing watchdog group is called the Web Standards Project (www.webstandards.org), and they're already making a difference in the browsers, which is good news to Web folk everywhere. The head of WSP is a fellow named Glenn Davis from San Francisco. He's on our side, so buy him a drink if you see him.

◆ Cycling through the Questions

To keep track of which question the user is currently on, we'll create a global variable called `currentQuestion` and set its initial value to 1. If the user presses the "Skip" button, `currentQuestion` will be advanced 1 without checking the user's answer. If the "Answer" button is pressed, a large function called `checkAnswer` is called that checks a small array to see if the user answered the question correctly. If not, then `checkAnswer` looks at another array to see if the answer warrants bringing up the suggestion layer and giving the user a choice if he or she wants to try again.

We'll introduce how to graphically chart the user's progress in Chapter 8, "A Really Interactive Quiz: Part Two."

The code for cycling through the questions, scoring right answers, and allowing second chances on certain questions is shown next. It's pretty complicated, so it's loaded with commentary inside the code and we'll break from the code list to discuss the more complex aspects.

```
<HTML>
<HEAD>

<TITLE>Shelley Biotechnologies - Quantum-Chaos rDNA
Compiler Interactive Quiz</TITLE>

<STYLE TYPE="text/css">
```

In the interest of saving space, we're only going to deal with the first four questions of the quiz in this code. However, the code is structured such that you could add as many questions as you wanted without trouble.

```
#question1
{
    position: absolute;
    top:100px;
    left: 50px;
    visibility: visible;
    width: 300px;
    color: purple;
}

#question2
{
    position: absolute;
    top: 100px;
    left: 50px;
    visibility: hidden;
    width: 300px;
    color: darkred;
}

#question3
{
    position: absolute;
    top: 100px;
    left: 50px;
    visibility: hidden;
    width: 300px;
    color: darkblue;
}

#question4
{
    position: absolute;
```

```
      top: 100px;
      left: 50px;
      visibility: hidden;
      width: 300px;
      color: #333333;
   }

   // This layer is what appears when the user is
   // given a second chance.
   #tryAgain
   {
      position: absolute;
      top: 20px;
      left: 100px;
      background-color: #CCCCCC;
      width: 200px;
      z-index: 10;
      visibility: hidden;
   }

   #score
   {
      position: absolute;
      top: 50px;
      left: 400px;
      border: solid gray 1px;
      padding: 10px;
   }

   #right
   {
      position: relative;
      font-size: 20pt;
      visibility: hidden;
   }

   #nope
   {
      position: relative;
      font-size: 20pt;
      visibility: hidden;
   }
```

We've grouped all the classes in one section, and we've created classes for styles that are only used once. This isn't necessary—we could code the style directly into the HTML—but we've
found it easier to deal with the code when all the style information is in one place.

```
.questionHeader
{
    font-size: 16pt;
    font-family: verdana, sans-serif;
    font-weight: bold;
}
.questionText { font-size: 12pt; font-family: verdana,
sans-serif; }
.questionChoices { font-weight: bold; font-size: 10pt;
font-family: verdana, sans-serif; }
.tryAgain {font-family: verdana, sans-serif; font-
weight: bold; font-size: 10pt; }
.score {font-size: 16pt; font-family: verdana, sans-
serif; font-weight: bold;}

// These classes are to control the color of the quiz
// choices, which is necessary when using tables
// in Netscape
.purple {color: purple}
.darkred {color: darkred}
.darkblue {color: darkblue}
.darkgray {color: #333333}

</STYLE>

<SCRIPT LANGUAGE="javascript">

   //Global variables

   // browser determination
   // (you've seen this before)

   var isNav, isIE
   if (parseInt(navigator.appVersion) >= 4)
   {
      if (navigator.appName == "Netscape")
      {
         isNav = true
         layerRef = "document.layers"
         styleRef = ""
      }
      else
      {
         isIE = true
         layerRef = "document.all"
         styleRef = ".style"
      }
   }
```

```
// keep track of which question is currently
// being answered
currentQuestion = 1

// keep track of score
score = 0

// keep track of whether the user is in the
// middle of trying to guess the same question
// again
tryAgain = "nope"

// record of correct answers
correctAnswer = new Array(9)

// the correct answers
correctAnswer[0] = "no"
correctAnswer[1] = "99%"
correctAnswer[2] = "40 million"
correctAnswer[3] = "3 stains"
correctAnswer[4] = "without"
correctAnswer[5] = "yes"
correctAnswer[6] = "above"
correctAnswer[7] = "separate"
correctAnswer[8] = "1987"
correctAnswer[9] = "you"

// keep track of which questions have been answered
answeredQuestions = new Array(10)
```

This next function presents the next question, whether the user's clicked on the "Skip" or "Answer" button. It hides the current question layer and shows the next question layer.

```
function nextQuestion ()
{
    // hide current question
    currentQuestionLayer = eval("'question' +
    currentQuestion")
    eval(layerRef + "['" + currentQuestionLayer + "']"
    + styleRef + ".visibility = 'hidden'")

    // increment which question is
    // the current question
    currentQuestion++

    // display the new question
    nextQuestionLayer = eval("'question' +
    currentQuestion")
```

```
    eval(layerRef + "['" + nextQuestionLayer + "']" +
    styleRef + ".visibility = 'visible'")
}

function checkAnswer()
{
    //
    // The Overall Plan of this Function:
    //
    // 1. determine user's answer
    // 2. check for another try
    // 3. assign points
    //

    //
    // 1. determine user's answer
    //

    currentObj = eval(layerRef + "['question" +
    currentQuestion + "'].document.question" +
    currentQuestion + "Form")
    if (currentQuestion == 1)
    {
        if ( currentObj.elements[1].checked == true)
        {
            userAnswer = "no"
        }
        else { userAnswer = "wrong answer" }
    }
    else if (currentQuestion == 2)
    {
        if ( currentObj.elements[2].checked == true)
        {
            userAnswer = "99%"
        }
        else { userAnswer = "wrong answer" }
    }
```

The user can get another chance to answer Question #3. There are four choices: choice 2 is the right one, and choice 4 is completely wrong. If the user chooses choice 4, he or she gets another chance. We keep track of whether the user is on a second guess or not with the variable tryAgain. If tryAgain is yes, that means the user is on the second guess. If the question is answered correctly, tryAgain becomes succeed. If the question is answered incorrectly again, tryAgain becomes fail. We'll use these values to determine the score later on. Remember, guessing correctly on a second guess will earn five points, while guessing incorrectly will cost five points.

```
else if (currentQuestion == 3)
{
   if ( currentObj.elements[1].checked == true)
   {
      userAnswer = "40 million"

      // see if they got it right on the second try
      if (tryAgain == "yes")
      {
         tryAgain = "succeed"
      }
   }
   else if (currentObj.elements[3].checked == true)
   // give them another try
   {
      userAnswer = "400 million"
      // make sure this isn't their
      // second guess already
      if (tryAgain != "yes")
      {
         tryAgain = "yes"
      }
      else // see if they guessed this one wrong
           // again (duh)
      {
         tryAgain = "fail"
      }
   }
   else
   {
      userAnswer = "wrong answer"

      // see if they got it wrong on the second try
      if (tryAgain == "yes")
      {
         tryAgain = "fail"
      }
   }

}
else if (currentQuestion == 4)
{
   if ( currentObj.elements[3].checked == true)
   {
      userAnswer = "3 stains"
   }
   else { userAnswer = "wrong answer" }
}
```

```
//
//  2. check for another try
//
```

This section displays the layer that gives the user another chance to guess again. The return statement jumps out of the `checkAnswer` function so that the code doesn't try to assign any points to the first guess.

```
if (tryAgain == "yes")
{
    eval( layerRef + "['tryAgain']" + styleRef +
    ".visibility = 'visible'")
    return
}

//
//  3. assign points
//

// The array counts from 0-9, while the
// questions go from 1-10. Thus, we have
// to take one from currentQuestion to
// call the right record in the array.
currentQuestionForArray = currentQuestion - 1
```

Further down in the HTML code, we introduce a new concept: nested layers. They look like this:

```
<DIV ID="score">
blah blah blah
    <DIV ID="right">blag</DIV>
    <DIV ID="nope">glab</DIV>
</DIV>
```

The layers `right` and `nope` can be treated as regular layers in DHTML, with a few tweaks to the code. To refer to the `right` layer in Netscape, use this syntax:

```
document.layers['score'].document.layers['right']
```

You just have to start over with the whole `document` thing. We'll see this type of syntax again in the next chapter. Using this syntax, we hide and display layers that tell the user whether he or she got the last question right or not.

```
if ( userAnswer ==
    correctAnswer[currentQuestionForArray] )
```

```
    {
        // let the user know they
        //got that one right
        eval( layerRef + "['score']." + layerRef +
        "['right']" + styleRef + ".visibility =
        'visible'")
        eval( layerRef + "['score']." + layerRef +
        "['nope']" + styleRef + ".visibility =
        'hidden'")

        // check if they got the question
        // right after a second try
        if (tryAgain == "succeed")
        {
            score += 5
            tryAgain = ""
        }
        else
        {
            score += 10
        }
        displayScore()
        answeredQuestions[currentQuestion] = "yes"

        nextQuestion()
    }
    else // they got it wrong
    {
        // let the user know they got that one wrong
        eval( layerRef + "['score']." + layerRef +
        "['right']" + styleRef + ".visibility =
        'hidden'")
        eval( layerRef + "['score']." + layerRef +
        "['nope']" + styleRef + ".visibility =
        'visible'")
        if (tryAgain == "fail")
        {
            score -= 5
            tryAgain = ""
        }
        displayScore()
        answeredQuestions[currentQuestion] = "yes"

        nextQuestion()
    }
}

function displayScore()
{
```

```
        document.layers['score'].document.score-
        Form.scoreBox.value = score
        return
    }

    //
    // this function deals with the user clicking on one
    // of the buttons on the tryAgain layer.
    function backToQuestion(direction)
    {
        // first, we hide the tryAgain layer
        eval( layerRef + "['tryAgain']" + styleRef +
        ".visibility = 'hidden'")

        // if the user decides to get the
        // question wrong and not take the gamble
        if (direction == "forward")
        {
            tryAgain = ""
            answeredQuestions[currentQuestion] = "yes"
            eval ( layerRef +
            "['progress'].document.progress" +
            currentQuestion + ".src = 'images/quiz/after_"
            + currentQuestion + ".gif'")
            nextQuestion ()
        }

        // If the user decides to give the question
        // another shot, we don't need to code anything
        // special. The "tryAgain" variable takes
        // care of that for us.

    }

</SCRIPT>

</HEAD>
```

Now let's look at the HTML. Again, we're only concerned with the first four questions in this sample.

```
<BODY BGCOLOR="#FFFFFF">

<DIV ID="score">
<SPAN CLASS="score">SCORE:</SPAN>
    <FORM NAME="scoreForm">
    <INPUT TYPE="text" NAME="scoreBox" SIZE="3">
    </FORM>
    <DIV ID="right">RIGHT!!</DIV>
```

```
    <DIV ID="nope">wrong-o</DIV>
</DIV>

<DIV ID="question1">
  <SPAN CLASS="questionHeader">Question #1</SPAN>
  <P>
  <SPAN CLASS="questionText">
        Will the Quantum-Chaos rDNA Compiler also
create the actual proteins that would be encoded from
the rDNA strands?
  </SPAN>
  </P>
  <FORM NAME="question1Form">
      <TABLE>
        <TR>
          <TD>
            <INPUT TYPE="radio" NAME="question1options">
          </TD>
```

The code shown next is where we deal with the troubles Netscape gives us when we use tables. Notice that you can nest <SPAN> tags within each other without any problems. However, if any of your nested <SPAN> tags have conflicting styles, test the page extensively to make sure the styles are inherited in the way you anticipate.

```
          <TD>
            <SPAN CLASS="questionChoices">
            <SPAN CLASS="purple">Yes</SPAN></SPAN>
          </TD>
        </TR>
        <TR>
          <TD>
            <INPUT TYPE="radio" NAME="question1options">
          </TD>
          <TD>
            <SPAN CLASS="questionChoices">
            <SPAN CLASS="purple">No</SPAN></SPAN>
          </TD>
        </TR>
      </TABLE>
      <P>
      <INPUT TYPE="button" VALUE="Skip" NAME="skip"
      onClick="nextQuestion()">
      <INPUT TYPE="button" VALUE="Answer"
      onClick="checkAnswer()">
  </FORM>
  </SPAN>
```

```
   </DIV>

   <DIV ID="question2">
      <SPAN CLASS="questionHeader">Question #2</SPAN>
      <P>
      <SPAN CLASS="questionText">
            What percentage of the rDNA strands harvested
by the Quantum-Chaos rDNA Compiler are unbroken?
      </SPAN>
      <FORM NAME="question2Form">
         <TABLE>
            <TR>
              <TD>
                 <INPUT TYPE="radio" NAME="question2options">
              </TD>
              <TD>
                 <SPAN CLASS="questionChoices">
                 <SPAN CLASS="darkred">100%</SPAN></SPAN>
              </TD>
            </TR>
            <TR>
              <TD>
                 <INPUT TYPE="radio" NAME="question2options">
              </TD>
              <TD>
                 <SPAN CLASS="questionChoices">
                 <SPAN CLASS="darkred">50%</SPAN></SPAN>
              </TD>
            </TR>
            <TR>
              <TD>
                 <INPUT TYPE="radio" NAME="question2options">
              </TD>
              <TD>
                 <SPAN CLASS="questionChoices">
                 <SPAN CLASS="darkred">99%</SPAN></SPAN>
              </TD>
            </TR>
         </TABLE>
         <P>
         <INPUT TYPE="button" VALUE="Skip" NAME="skip"
         onClick="nextQuestion()">
         <INPUT TYPE="button" VALUE="Answer"
         onClick="checkAnswer()">
      </FORM>
   </DIV>

   <DIV ID="question3">
      <SPAN CLASS="questionHeader">Question #3</SPAN>
```

```
<P>
<SPAN CLASS="questionText">
        How many actual complete strands of rDNA are
typically harvested by each run of the Q-C rDNA
Compiler?
</SPAN>
<FORM NAME="question3Form">
    <TABLE>
        <TR>
            <TD>
                <INPUT TYPE="radio" NAME="question3options">
            </TD>
            <TD>
                <SPAN CLASS="questionChoices">
                <SPAN CLASS="darkblue">1 million</SPAN>
                </SPAN>
            </TD>
        </TR>
        <TR>
            <TD>
                <INPUT TYPE="radio" NAME="question3options">
            </TD>
            <TD>
                <SPAN CLASS="questionChoices">
                <SPAN CLASS="darkblue">40 million</SPAN>
                </SPAN>
            </TD>
        </TR>
        <TR>
            <TD>
                <INPUT TYPE="radio" NAME="question3options">
            </TD>
            <TD>
                <SPAN CLASS="questionChoices">
                <SPAN CLASS="darkblue">400 million</SPAN>
                </SPAN>
            </TD>
        </TR>
        <TR>
            <TD>
                <INPUT TYPE="radio" NAME="question3options">
            </TD>
            <TD>
                <SPAN CLASS="questionChoices">
                <SPAN CLASS="darkblue">2 billion</SPAN>
                </SPAN>
            </TD>
        </TR>
    </TABLE>
```

```
            <P>
            <INPUT TYPE="button" VALUE="Skip" NAME="skip"
            onClick="nextQuestion()">
            <INPUT TYPE="button" VALUE="Answer"
            onClick="checkAnswer()">
         </FORM>
   </DIV>

   <DIV ID="question4">
      <SPAN CLASS="questionHeader">Question #4</SPAN>
      <P>
      <SPAN CLASS="questionText">
            How many stains should you perform to confirm
   that you have the proper rDNA configuration?
      </SPAN>
      <FORM NAME="question4Form">
         <TABLE>
            <TR>
              <TD>
                 <INPUT TYPE="radio" NAME="question4options">
              </TD>
              <TD>
                 <SPAN CLASS="questionChoices">
                 <SPAN CLASS="darkgray">None</SPAN>
                 </SPAN>
              </TD>
            </TR>
            <TR>
              <TD>
                 <INPUT TYPE="radio" NAME="question4options">
              </TD>
              <TD>
                 <SPAN CLASS="questionChoices">
                 <SPAN CLASS="darkgray">1 stain</SPAN>
                 </SPAN>
              </TD>
            </TR>
            <TR>
              <TD>
                 <INPUT TYPE="radio" NAME="question4options">
              </TD>
              <TD>
                 <SPAN CLASS="questionChoices">
                 <SPAN CLASS="darkgray">2 stains</SPAN>
                 </SPAN>
              </TD>
            </TR>
            <TR>
              <TD>
```

```
                <INPUT TYPE="radio" NAME="question4options">
            </TD>
            <TD>
                <SPAN CLASS="questionChoices">
                <SPAN CLASS="darkgray">3 stains</SPAN>
                </SPAN>
            </TD>
        </TR>
    </TABLE>
    <P>
    <INPUT TYPE="button" VALUE="Skip" NAME="skip"
    onClick="nextQuestion()">
    <INPUT TYPE="button" VALUE="Answer"
    onClick="checkAnswer()">
    </FORM>
</DIV>

<!--
    The layer that lets the user decide whether they
    want another chance or not.
-->
<DIV ID="tryAgain">
<TABLE BGCOLOR="#CCCCCC" WIDTH="300"
CELLPADDING="10"><TR><TD BGCOLOR="#CCCCCC">
    <SPAN CLASS="tryAgain">
    Good grief and sorry. You're not even close.
    <P>
    We'll let you guess again. If you guess right, you'll
get five points. But if you guess wrong, we'll take five
points off your score.
    <P>
    Are you ready for it?
    </SPAN>
    <FORM NAME="tryAgainForm">
        <INPUT TYPE="button" VALUE="No way. Next question,
        please" onClick="backToQuestion('forward')">
        <INPUT TYPE="button" VALUE="Yeah! I'll go for it!"
        onClick="backToQuestion('stay')">
    </FORM>
    </TD></TR></TABLE>
</DIV>

</BODY>
</HTML>
```

So that's the first part of the quiz. The user moves through the questions, either answering them or skipping them. For Question #3, if the fourth choice is selected, the user is given another chance and the point stakes are increased a little bit.

In the next chapter, we'll implement the Quiz Progress Chart, which makes the quiz much easier and more interesting to move through. We'll also implement a feature that shows some links to other sections of the Shelley Web site based on the user's score.

RECAP

We've looked at another way to implement many of the concepts and techniques discussed earlier in the book, including classes, positioning, and layer visibility based on user input. Our example of the interactive quiz is significantly more advanced than the other examples, and mastery of this project's code will put you into the Power User category for DHTML.

We also had a look at nested layers and how to refer to them in DHTML.

ADVANCED PROJECTS

There isn't any advanced work for you in this chapter. The next chapter continues to build on this project, so just continue on and check out the advanced work at the end of Chapter 8.

8 A Really Interactive Quiz: Part Two

IN THIS CHAPTER

- Introduction
- Quiz Progress and Navigation
- Recap
- Book Recap
- Advanced Projects

◆ Introduction

We left the interactive quiz in an incomplete, but workable, state. Users can answer questions, they can skip questions, and if their answer is totally off, they're occasionally given a second chance to guess right. Their overall score is tallied at the end of every question. However, a few things are missing from our working version.

The first thing we're missing is a way for users to move through the quiz in a nonlinear way. For example, there's no way for users to go back and answer what they skipped. If they forgot which question they skipped, there's no way for them to find out which one it was. If they forgot that there are 10 questions, they're out of luck until they finish the quiz. None of the features are necessary for a decent quiz, but your job isn't to create a decent quiz; you're supposed to create a quiz that will make people go "Wow!" and tell their friends about it.

The second feature we're missing is the ability of the code to realize when the user has reached the end of the quiz. When the user finishes the quiz, we want the code to spit out some links to other sections of the Shelley site. These links will be based on the user's score—low scores will get links to the more fundamental parts of the Web site. High quiz scores will yield links to more technically advanced sections of the site.

◆ Quiz Progress and Navigation

Let's look at the details of how we want users to navigate their way through our quiz. We want it to be intuitive, nonlinear, and pretty cool.

What Should Happen

The Quiz Progress section will appear as shown in Figure 8–1.

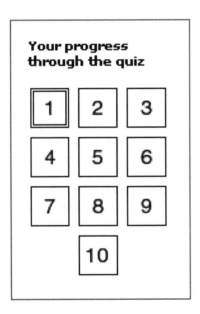

FIGURE 8–1 The Quiz Progress section the user sees when he or she begins the quiz

There's a box for every question in the quiz. Questions that haven't been answered yet are black numbers against a white background with a black border. The current question is highlighted by a double blue border.

As the user progresses through the quiz, the boxes become gray, much like menu items that cannot be used (see Figure 8–2).

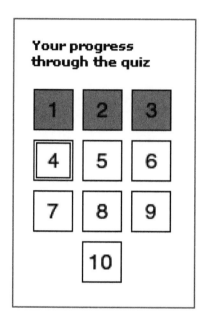

FIGURE 8–2 The Quiz Progress section after the user has answered three questions

Simply charting progress is nice, but we're going to code actual navigation into these boxes. If the user is on Question #3 and decides to see what Question #10 looks like, he or she can just click on box #10. Question #10 appears and the Question #3 box remains white, because that question hasn't been answered yet.

Being able to skip around and answer any question complicates the navigation, as you might imagine. Suppose the user answered the first two questions, skipped Question #3, but answered the next four questions. That puts the user at Question #8. He or she decides it's time to answer Question #3, clicks on box #3 and answers the question. The code needs to understand that the next question is not Question #4, because the user already answered that question. The questions should go straight from 3 to 8, so we need some code to decide which question the user should be shown next.

Also, once a user answers a question, he or she shouldn't be able to go back to that question. Therefore, the Quiz Progress section can't allow a user to go back to a question that's already been answered.

Quiz Progress Images and Code

For each box in the Quiz Progress section, there are really three images:

1. The box with the blue double border for the current question (filename looks like `current_1.gif`).

2. The box with the white background for unanswered questions (filename looks like `before_8.gif`).

3. The box with a gray background for answered questions (filename looks like `after_4.gif`).

This yields a total of 30 images. These images will be swapped with plain ol' image replacement that you see in mouse rollovers on many Web sites. You could place each image on its own nested layer and replace each layer as the questions change, but we found that image replacement in this case is faster, easier to code, and simpler to build than a fancy DHTML solution.

Our layer declaration for this section looks like this:

```
#progress
{
    position: absolute;
    top: 200px;
    left: 400px;
    border: solid gray 1px;
    padding: 10px;
}
```

See anything new? We haven't talked about the `border` or `padding` attributes yet. The `border` attribute lets you draw a customized box around a layer. The three values used here (`solid gray 1px`) tell the browser that the border should be a solid line, gray, and 1 pixel wide. See Appendix A "CSS Style Attribute Reference," for more options for this attribute.

The `padding` attribute is also new. A layer's padding is defined as empty space between the content of the layer (such as images, text, and form elements) and the actual edge of the layer. Thus, using `padding` creates some extra space between images in this layer and the border.

Here's what the layer content code looks like:

```
<DIV ID="progress">
    <SPAN CLASS="questionChoices">Your
    progress<BR>through the quiz</SPAN>
    <BR><BR>
    <A HREF="javascript:questionJump(1)">
    <IMG SRC="images/quiz/current_1.gif" NAME="progress1"
    WIDTH="31" HEIGHT="31" BORDER="0" HSPACE="2"
    VSPACE="2"></A>
    <A HREF="javascript:questionJump(2)">
    <IMG SRC="images/quiz/before_2.gif" NAME="progress2"
    WIDTH="31" HEIGHT="31" BORDER="0" HSPACE="2"
    VSPACE="2"></A>
    <A HREF="javascript:questionJump(3)">
    <IMG SRC="images/quiz/before_3.gif" NAME="progress3"
    WIDTH="31" HEIGHT="31" BORDER="0" HSPACE="2"
    VSPACE="2"></A>
    <BR>
    <A HREF="javascript:questionJump(4)">
    <IMG SRC="images/quiz/before_4.gif" NAME="progress4"
    WIDTH="31" HEIGHT="31" BORDER="0" HSPACE="2"
    VSPACE="2"></A>
    <A HREF="javascript:questionJump(5)">
    <IMG SRC="images/quiz/before_5.gif" NAME="progress5"
    WIDTH="31" HEIGHT="31" BORDER="0" HSPACE="2"
    VSPACE="2"></A>
    <A HREF="javascript:questionJump(6)">
    <IMG SRC="images/quiz/before_6.gif" NAME="progress6"
    WIDTH="31" HEIGHT="31" BORDER="0" HSPACE="2"
    VSPACE="2"></A>
    <BR>
    <A HREF="javascript:questionJump(7)">
    <IMG SRC="images/quiz/before_7.gif" NAME="progress7"
    WIDTH="31" HEIGHT="31" BORDER="0" HSPACE="2"
    VSPACE="2"></A>
    <A HREF="javascript:questionJump(8)">
    <IMG SRC="images/quiz/before_8.gif" NAME="progress8"
    WIDTH="31" HEIGHT="31" BORDER="0" HSPACE="2"
    VSPACE="2"></A>
    <A HREF="javascript:questionJump(9)">
    <IMG SRC="images/quiz/before_9.gif" NAME="progress9"
    WIDTH="31" HEIGHT="31" BORDER="0" HSPACE="2"
```

```
VSPACE="2"></A>
<BR>
<A HREF="javascript:questionJump(10)">
<IMG SRC="images/quiz/before_10.gif"
NAME="progress10" WIDTH="31" HEIGHT="31" BORDER="0"
HSPACE="40" VSPACE="2"></A>
</DIV>
```

Say the user sees this configuration: the quiz just started, box #1 is shown as the current box, and the rest are just simple boxes with numbers in them. The user decides he or she must see Question #6, and clicks the image and calls `questionJump(6)`.

Here's what that function looks like:

```
function questionJump(questionNumber)
{
    // make sure the question clicked on
    // hasn't been answered yet
    if (answeredQuestions[questionNumber] != "yes")
    {

        // hide current question layer
        eval(layerRef + "['question" + currentQuestion +
        "']" + styleRef + ".visibility = 'hidden'")

        // make the clicked-on question image visible
        eval(layerRef + "['question" + nextQuestion + "']"
        + styleRef + ".visibility = 'visible'")

        // image replacement:
        // change the current question image
        // to the unanswered version
        eval ( layerRef + "['progress'].document.progress"
        + currentQuestion + ".src = 'images/quiz/before_"
        + currentQuestion + ".gif'")

        // image replacement:
        // change the clicked-on question image
        // to the current version
        eval ( layerRef + "['progress'].document.progress"
        + questionNumber + ".src = 'images/quiz/current_"
        + questionNumber + ".gif'")

        //update the currentQuestion variable
        currentQuestion = questionNumber
    }
}
```

This function is responsible for determining whether an image is clickable or not, which is determined by:

```
if (answeredQuestions[questionNumber] != "yes")
```

If the question has already been answered, nothing happens when the user clicks on the image.

This isn't all that's involved in the Quiz Progress section. Images need to be updated every time a user answers a question or skips a question. If a question is answered, the image for that question needs to turn gray; the code needs to see which question is the next one, display that question, and make that image the current version. If a question is skipped, the code goes through the same process, but it displays the skipped question as unanswered.

We can accomplish much of this by altering the nextQuestion function.

```
function nextQuestion ()
{
```
1.
```
    // if the previous question was skipped, set the
    // question's progress image to "before" setting
    if ( !answeredQuestions[currentQuestion] )
    {
        eval( layerRef + "['progress'].document.progress"
        + currentQuestion + ".src = 'images/quiz/before_"
        + currentQuestion + ".gif'")
    }

    currentQuestionLayer = eval("'question'
    + currentQuestion")
    eval(layerRef + "['" + currentQuestionLayer + "']"
    + styleRef + ".visibility = 'hidden'")
```
2.
```
    currentQuestion++

    //check to see if next question was answered already
    while ( currentQuestion < 11)
    {
        if (answeredQuestions[currentQuestion] == "yes")
        {
            currentQuestion++
        }
        else { break }
    }

    nextQuestionLayer = eval("'question'
    + currentQuestion")
```

```
        eval(layerRef + "['" + nextQuestionLayer + "']"
        + styleRef + ".visibility = 'visible'")
```

3.
```
        // set next image to current
        eval( layerRef + "['progress'].document.progress"
        + currentQuestion + ".src = 'images/quiz/current_"
        + currentQuestion + ".gif'")
    }
```

HOW THE CODE WORKS

1. The first thing we do is see if the user answered the current question. If not, that means the user skipped it and the Quiz Progress image should be changed from a current version (double blue border) to an unanswered version (single black border).

2. Next, we increment the `currentQuestion` variable and then see if that question was answered or not. We use a `while` loop to cycle through all the possibilities. If the question we're looking at has already been answered, we increment `currentQuestion` by 1 and continue checking. If the question hasn't been answered, we break out of the loop and continue with the function.

3. After we display the correct question, we change that question's image to the current version (double blue border).

You may have noticed that we haven't come across any code that changes an answered question's image to the answered version (black border, gray background). We implement this code in the `checkAnswer` function, right before we assign points:

```
    //
    // 3. Advance progress check
    //
    // set current progress to after
    eval ( layerRef + "['progress'].document.progress"
    + currentQuestion + ".src = 'images/quiz/after_"
    + currentQuestion + ".gif'")
```

This completes the code for the functionality of answering questions.

The End of the Quiz

When the user reaches the end of the quiz, he or she needs to be recognized and congratulated, even if he or she missed everything. The user should also be shown some links according to how well he or she performed on the quiz. All users will be shown the same links, but they'll be in different orders, and different links will be emphasized. If most of the questions were missed, the links will focus on introductory sections of the site. If the user did fine, all links will be given equal weight and the user can choose which ones are most important.

To determine whether the user has reached the end of the quiz, insert this code snippet in the checkAnswer function:

```
function nextQuestion ()
{
    // if the previous question was skipped, set the
    // question's progress image to "before" setting
    if ( !answeredQuestions[currentQuestion] )
    {
        eval( layerRef + "['progress'].document.progress"
        + currentQuestion + ".src = 'images/quiz/before_"
        + currentQuestion + ".gif'")
    }


    currentQuestionLayer = eval("'question'
    + currentQuestion")
    eval(layerRef + "['" + currentQuestionLayer + "']"
    + styleRef + ".visibility = 'hidden'")

    currentQuestion++

    //check to see if next question was answered already
    while ( currentQuestion < 11)
    {
        if (answeredQuestions[currentQuestion] == "yes")
        {
            currentQuestion++
        }
        else { break }
    }

    if (currentQuestion == 11)
    {
        quizFinished()
        return
    }

    nextQuestionLayer = eval("'question'
    + currentQuestion")
```

```
    eval(layerRef + "['" + nextQuestionLayer + "']"
    + styleRef + ".visibility = 'visible'")

    // set next image to current
    eval( layerRef + "['progress'].document.progress"
    + currentQuestion + ".src = 'images/quiz/current_"
    + currentQuestion + ".gif'")


    // layerName = eval("'question' + currentQuestion")
    // document.layers['debug'].document.debugForm
    // .textBox.value = layerName
}
```

Since the quiz has only 10 questions, if currentQuestion has reached 11, we're done. We create a function called quizFinished that displays the appropriate set of links, and then we return, which jumps us out of the DHTML and waits for the user to do something (hopefully, click one of the links presented). Here's the quizFinished function:

```
function quizFinished ()
{
    if (score < 30) // new user
    {
        eval ( layerRef + "['endQuizNovice']" + styleRef
        + ".visibility = 'visible'"  )
    }
    else if (score < 70) // intermediate user
    {
        eval ( layerRef + "['endQuizIntermediate']"
        + styleRef + ".visibility = 'visible'"  )
    }
    else // some professor
    {
        eval ( layerRef + "['endQuizAdvanced']"
        + styleRef + ".visibility = 'visible'"  )
    }
}
```

This is a pretty simple function: depending on the user's score, any one of three layers is displayed.

RECAP

The only truly new things we learned in this chapter are the border and padding attributes, which affect the space around a layer's viewable area. We hope that walking through the Quiz Progress section and coding the finale of the quiz were also helpful in showing you more ways to implement DHTML.

BOOK RECAP

You did it! You just learned DHTML! This books burns through a lot of information at a fast and furious pace, so congratulate yourself for making it this far. We hope the material was presented in a manner that was useful to you.

From time to time, we strongly recommend you browse through the appendices of this book, especially Appendix A. We've built a list of all the attributes that work in both the Netscape and Internet Explorer (IE) version 4 browsers. We even learned a few new things in compiling this list, so you may as well.

<PLUG TYPE= "SHAMELESS">
Much of what is possible in DHTML is also possible, with a smaller file size, using Macromedia's Flash technology. Pick up the Flash book in this series by Lynn Kyle—it's great.

Also, the amount of functionality possible on Web pages is multiplied a hundredfold with scripting languages and using CGI. So, of course, you should look at our book on the immensely popular Perl language, *Essential Perl 5 for Web Professionals*, as well as our forthcoming books on ASP, Microsoft's popular scripting technology, and PHP, a powerful up-and-coming scripting language that's similar to Perl but easier to learn.

There are about 4000 other books in this series, all damn good. Really.
</PLUG>

ADVANCED PROJECTS

When we look for the next open question, we don't see if there are any questions that went unanswered. Suppose the user just answered Question #10 and only Question #5 was unanswered? How would you develop code to check that?

A CSS Style Attribute Reference

This reference includes only the style attributes that work on both Netscape and Internet Explorer (IE) version 4 browsers. Generally, IE has many more features than Netscape because it was released later, and the latest CSS specification (known as CSS2) also defines many features that neither browser has. The CSS2 features that aren't implemented by either browser, and the features that are IE-only, are not included here. We're also skipping attributes that do work in both browsers, but work so wildly differently that they have different effects. We're doing this because you should be coding your pages to work in both browsers.

As for the next generation of browsers, it looks like Mozilla (for Netscape 5.0) will fully conform to accepted W3C CSS standards, when the open source browser is finally finished (which is worth waiting for, in our opinion). Unfortunately, Internet Explorer 5.0 definitely doesn't conform to these standards, so it'll be a longer wait for us developer types before we can write one script that works everywhere.

The attributes fall into six categories:

- Box Property
- Color and Background
- Classification
- Font
- Text
- Position

◆ Box Property Attributes

border-top
border-bottom
border-right
border-left

Using these four attributes, you can set the style, color, and width of any of the four sides of your border. Any values you don't explicitly set stay with their initial values.

Syntax

```
border-top: border-top-width border-top-style color
border-bottom: border-bottom-width border-bottom-style
color
border-right: border-right-width border-right-style
color
border-left: border-left-width border-left-style  color
```

Values

For the border width and style values, see the following example. For acceptable color values, see Appendix B, "Miscellaneous Reference."

Example

```
P
{
    border-top: ridge 5px darkred;
    border-bottom: ridge 5px darkred;
    border-right: ridge 2px darkred;
    border-left: ridge 2px darkred;
}
```

border-color

You can set the color of all four sides of your border with this attribute. Netscape allows only one value, which applies to all four sides. IE and CSS2 allow you to specify each side individually.

Syntax

```
border-color: color {1-4 values}
```

Values

Netscape allows only one color value.

IE allows up to four different color values that have the counter-intuitive effects listed in Table A–1.

TABLE A–1 Color Values and Effects for `border-color`

Number of Values	Effect
1	Sets all four border sides to the same color.
2	Top and bottom get the first color value, right and left get the second color value.
3	Top gets the first color value, right and left borders get the second color value, and the bottom gets the third color value.
4	Sets the borders in clockwise fashion: top, right, bottom, and left.

Examples

```
H2 { border-color: red blue #3366FF rgb(0%, 95%, 30%) }
P { border-color: green coral }
```

border-top-color
border-right-color
border-bottom-color
border-left-color

Each of these attributes sets the color of an individual border element. See the `border-color` attribute to see how to set these colors in a single statement.

Syntax

```
border-top-color: color
border-right-color: color
border-bottom-color: color
border-left-color: color
```

Values

Any valid color value is acceptable (see the "Colors" section in Appendix B).

Examples

```
H1
{
    border-top-color: blue;
```

```
    border-right-color: lightblue
}

P
{
    border-bottom-color: rgb (0, 51, 153);
    border-left-color: rgb (14%, 33%, 89%)
}
```

border-style

This is another border attribute that allows you to determine the styles of the border elements in either the same or different styles. Netscape allows for only a single value, while IE allows for up to four.

Syntax

```
border-style: borderStyle {1-4}
```

Values

Not all of the styles in CSS2 are recognized by the browsers. Here's a list of styles that work in Netscape and IE:

```
double
groove
inset
none
outset
ridge
solid
```

The number of values determines which sides receive which border styles, as shown in Table A–2.

TABLE A–2 Color Values and Effects for `border-style`

Number of Values	Effect
1	Sets all four border sides to the same style.
2	Top and bottom get the first style, right and left get the second style.
3	Top gets the first style, right and left borders get the second style, and the bottom gets the third style.
4	Sets the border styles in clockwise fashion: top, right, bottom, and left.

Examples

```
P { border-style: ridge solid }
H1 { border-style: ridge none solid none }
```

border-top-style
border-right-style
border-bottom-style
border-left-style

Each of these attributes sets the style of an individual border element. See the `border-style` attribute to see how to set these styles in a single statement.

Syntax

```
border-top-style: borderStyle
border-right-style: borderStyle
border-bottom-style: borderStyle
border-left-style: borderStyle
```

Values

Not all of the styles in CSS2 are recognized by the browsers. Here's a list of styles that work in Netscape and IE:

```
double
groove
inset
none
outset
ridge
solid
```

Examples

```
H1
{
    border-top-style: ridge;
    border-right-style: solid;
}

P
{
    border-bottom-style: groove;
    border-left-style: double;
}
```

border-width

This attribute allows you to set the width of all the borders of an element in one statement, much like the `border-color` and `border-style` attributes.

Syntax

```
border-width: thin | medium | thick | length {1,4}
```

Values

The three constants—`thin`, `medium`, and `thick`—allow the browser to choose the border thickness for you. You can determine the exact width for yourself. For acceptable length units, see the "Measurement Units" section in Appendix B.

If you opt for an exact measurement, you can enter up to four values. Based on how many values you enter, certain sides of the border are affected, as shown in Table A–3.

TABLE A–3 Width Values and Effects for `border-width`

Number of Values	Effect
1	Sets all four border sides to the same style.
2	Top and bottom get the first style, right and left get the second style.
3	Top gets the first style, right and left borders get the second style, and the bottom gets the third style.
4	Sets the border styles in clockwise fashion: top, right, bottom, and left.

Examples

```
P {border-width: 5px 3px 5px;}
DIV {border-width: thin;}
B {border-width: 10mm 20mm 10mm 15mm;}
```

border-top-width
border-right-width
border-bottom-width
border-left-width

Each of these attributes sets the width of an individual border element. See the `border-width` attribute to see how to set these widths in a single statement.

Syntax

```
border-top-width:    thin | medium | thick | length
border-right-width:  thin | medium | thick | length
border-bottom-width: thin | medium | thick | length
border-left-width:   thin | medium | thick | length
```

Values

The three constants—thin, medium, and thick—allow the browser to choose the border thickness for you. For an exact width, you can determine the length for yourself. For acceptable length units, see the "Measurement Units" section in Appendix B.

Examples

```
H1
{
    border-top-width: 3px;
    border-right-width: 6px;
}

P
{
    border-bottom-width: .25in;
    border-left-width: .35in;
}
```

clear

This is a little tricky to describe. clear defines whether an element can be displayed in the same horizontal band as a floating element (see the float attribute later in this appendix). Since float usually has a value of left or right, you'll want your clear value to have the same value. If clear has a value other than none, the element will be rendered at the beginning of the next available line below the floating element. However, since Netscape and IE don't render the float element in the same way, you'll probably avoid both the float and clear attributes for the time being.

Syntax

```
clear: right | left | both | none
```

Values

Any of the preceding four values: right, left, both, or none.

Examples

```
<IMG SRC="images/biolab.gif" HEIGHT="40" WIDTH="100"
STYLE="float:left">
<H2 STYLE="clear:left">Get a Portable BioLab today!"</H2>
```

float

Essentially, this attribute acts as an element alignment that allows other content to wrap around it. It's often used on an image so that text wraps around it. However, there are some completely irreconcilable differences between Netscape and IE, so we recommend ignoring this attribute for the time being.

Syntax

```
float: alignment | none
```

Values
The alignment can be either right or left.

Examples

```
IMG { float: left }
```

margin

This attribute can set the widths of the invisible margins along all four sides of an element with a single statement. Margins extend beyond the visible edge of an element, and are useful in setting extra empty space around an element.

Syntax

```
margin: thickness | auto {1,4}
```

Values
The *thickness* of the margin can be regular lengths (see the "Measurement Units" section in Appendix B). You can also opt to enter up to four values for the size of the margins. The number of values you enter affects which sides accept those values, as shown in Table A–4.

Examples

```
P { margin: 20px 15 px 20px;}
```

TABLE A–4 Style Values and Effects for `border-style`

Number of Values	Effect
1	Sets all four border sides to the same style.
2	Top and bottom get the first style, right and left get the second style.
3	Top gets the first style, right and left borders get the second style, and the bottom gets the third style.
4	Sets the border styles in clockwise fashion: top, right, bottom, and left.

margin-top
margin-right
margin-bottom
margin-left

These attributes set the width of a certain margin of an element. The margin is the invisible space that extends beyond the viewable area, like the margins on this page. You can set all four margins in one statement with the `margin` attribute.

Syntax

```
margin-top: thickness | auto
margin-right: thickness | auto
margin-bottom: thickness | auto
margin-left: thickness | auto
```

Values

The thickness can be lengths (see the "Measurement Units" section in Appendix B), percentages of the next most outermost element size, or `auto`, which is the browser default.

Examples

```
H1
{
   margin-top: 3px;
   margin-right: 16px;
}

P
{
   margin-bottom: .25in;
```

```
    margin-left: .35in;
}
```

padding

Padding is the space that occurs between the edge of the element and the beginning of its border. Increasing the padding around an element adds space inside of its border, so the border has a larger area to cover. Unlike margin, increasing an element's padding increases the size of the element, but the size of the content remains unaffected. Be aware that Netscape adds its own 3-pixel padding around your content, and there's nothing you can do about it; any padding you specify is added to the 3-pixel padding that's already there.

Syntax

```
padding: thickness {1,4}
```

Values

You can enter up to four values. These values can be lengths (see the "Measurement Units" section in Appendix B), or percentages of the next outermost element size. The number of values you enter determine which sides get affected, as shown in Table A–5.

TABLE A–5 Number of Values and Effects for padding

Number of Values	Effect
1	Sets all four border sides to the same style.
2	Top and bottom get the first style, right and left get the second style.
3	Top gets the first style, right and left borders get the second style, and the bottom gets the third style.
4	Sets the border styles in clockwise fashion: top, right, bottom, and left.

Examples

```
P {border-color: red; padding: 5px 10px; }
```

padding-top
padding-right
padding-bottom
padding-left

These attributes set the width of a certain padding of an element. Padding is the space between the content block and the inner edge of the element's border. You can set all four padding sides in one statement with the padding attribute.

Syntax

```
padding-top: thickness
padding-right: thickness
padding-bottom: thickness
padding-left: thickness
```

Values

You can enter up to four values. These values can be lengths (see the "Measurement Units" section in Appendix B), or percentages of the next outermost element size.

Examples

```
H1
{
    padding-top: 30px;
    padding-right: 10px;
}

P
{
    padding-bottom: 4pt;
    padding-left: 6pt;
}
```

◆ Color and Background Attributes

background-color

This sets the background color for the element. One thing to be aware of if you're setting the background color of a <P> in order for the text to have color behind it: The background color will only occur under the actual letters, not in a neat rectangle.

Syntax

```
background-color: color
```

Values

Any valid color reference will work. See the "Colors" section in Appendix B.

Examples

```
P { background-color: yellow; }
```

background-image

This sets the background image for the element (not the whole page). If you set a background color as well as an image, the color will appear only if the image fails to load. However, transparent pixels in a GIF image will allow the background color to show through.

Syntax

```
background-image: url | none
```

Values

You can point to any image that's local or on the Web, as long as you place the path and filename inside a url() wrapper. Use the none option only to avoid an image from being loaded.

Examples

```
H2 { background-image: url( images/welcome.gif ); }
```

color

This defines the text color of an element. It can also control the color along the edges of some form elements, like submit and radio buttons. However, this sort of control is inconsistent across browsers, so test carefully.

Syntax

```
color: color
```

Values

Any valid color reference will work. See the "Colors" section in Appendix B for details.

Examples

```
B { color: darkblue; }
```

◆ Classification Attributes

display

This is an odd attribute that can be used for many things. It determines whether an element should be rendered in the page, and whether space should be reserved for it on the page. CSS2 also allows for a further definition of the element: `block`, `inline`, `run-in`, `table-row`, and more. However, these further classifications aren't supported by IE or Netscape, so the only value you'll probably ever use is `none`. Note that this differs from making a layer visible: `hidden`, because hiding a layer still reserves space for the element.

Syntax

```
display: display-type
```

Values

Any of these values: `none` | `block` | `compact` | `inline` | `inline-table` | `list-item` | `run-in` | `table` | `table-caption` | `table-cell` | `table-column-group` | `table-footer-group` | `table-header-group` | `table-row` | `table-row-group`.

Examples

```
hidden { display: none; }
```

list-style-type

This sets the kind of marker that accompanies a list item. These markers are in two categories: one is used with UL lists and can be a filled disc, an empty circle, or a square (empty in Macs, filled in Windows). The other set is used with OL lists, and all the items are in a sequence. This attribute can vary among the browsers a bit unpredictably, so test it thoroughly.

Syntax

```
list-style-type: styleType
```

Values

For UL-type lists, the possibilities are `circle` | `disc` | `square`. For OL-type lists, the options are `decimal` | `lower-alpha` | `lower-roman` | `upper-alpha` | `upper-roman`. Examples of the OL-type markers are listed in Table A–6.

TABLE A–6 Marker Types and Examples for `list-style-type`

Marker Type	Example
decimal	1, 2, 3
lower-alpha	a, b, c
lower-roman	i, ii, iii
upper-alpha	A, B, C
upper-roman	I, II, III

Examples

```
OL { list-style-type: upper-roman }
UL {list-style-type: square }
```

◆ *Font Attributes*

font-family

You can set an element's font with this attribute. One or more fonts (or "font families") can be set up with a space-delimited list. A font family may consist of several font definitions. For example, Helvetica is a font family, but there are several fonts within the Helvetica family, including special fonts for bold and italic Helvetica letters.

When you specify more than one font family, the browser looks at the user's system and sees if it has the first font you've specified. If not, the browser moves to the second font family and sees if the user's system has that font. Thus, you should list your fonts in order from most esoteric to more generic. For example, if your font list includes Arial, Bad Girl, and Avenir Black, list them like this: Bad Girl, Avenir Black, and Arial.

Syntax

```
font-family: fontFamily1 fontFamily2 …
```

Values

Any font can be listed, as long as there's a space in between the names. If the font name itself uses two words or more, enclose the name of the font in double quotes. Generic family names are `serif | sans-serif | cursive | fantasy | monospace`.

Examples

```
P {font-family: "Bad Girl" "Avenir Black" arial sans-serif}
```

font-size

This attribute determines the size of text. The size can be determined in several ways: by length (9pt, 12pt, 2em), by absolute sizes (x-small, large), by relative sizes with words and percentages (larger, smaller, 75%, 150%). Since Macs and Windows render fonts in different sizes, we recommend using only points. It still won't give you exactly the same size on both platforms, but it's as close as you'll get.

Syntax

```
font-size: length | absoluteSize | relativeSize |
percentage
```

Values

For all the length options, see the "Measurement Units" section in Appendix B. You have many options, but we recommend you use points unless you have a great reason not to. The absolute sizes are xx-small | x-small | small | medium | large | x-large | xx-large. Relative sizes are smaller | larger. For percentages, just use a number and the % sign.

Examples

```
P { font-size: larger; }
H1 { font-size: 24pt; }
B { font-size: x-large; }
I { font-size: 150%; }
```

font-style

This attribute lets you render fonts in italic. Technically, the other options are normal and oblique, but oblique doesn't work in Netscape and IE renders it as italic.

Syntax

```
font-style: style
```

Values

You can use normal | italic | oblique.

Examples

```
EM { font-style: italic; }
```

font-weight

Set the boldness (weight) of your text with this attribute. CSS2 allows more options for text weight than browsers can handle.

Syntax

```
font-weight: weight
```

Values

The relative values you can use are `bold` | `bolder` | `lighter` | `normal`. You can also use numerals, starting from 100 and going to 900 in increments of 100. A value of 400 or 500 (depending on the font) is normal boldness, and what you and I know as bold is 700. The numbers are more for when you're sending this page to a printer and are not useful now to Web designers.

Examples

```
B { font-weight: bold }
I { font-style: italic; font-weight: lighter }
```

◆ *Text Attributes*

line-height

Stay away from this one if you can. This attribute affects the height of the line containing one line of text. If Netscape and IE rendered `line-height` in the same way, or even had the same set of problems in dealing with this attribute, this would be a great attribute. You can still use it successfully, but it requires extensive testing.

Syntax

```
line-height: normal | number | length | percentage
```

Values

A value of `normal` leaves the text as it would be without stylesheets. A pure number acts as a multiplier for the font size. The length acts as an absolute measure of line height. A percentage acts as a multiplier for the font size of the element.

Examples

```
P { line-height: 2em; }
DIV { line-height: 150%; }
SPAN { line-height: normal; }
P.tall {line-height:  2.1; }
```

text-align

This determines the horizontal alignment of text in an element. It has a possible value of justify, but the browsers implement it inconsistently, so avoid justify.

Syntax

```
text-align: alignment
```

Values

You can use left | center | right.

Examples

```
P { text-align: left; }
DIV { text-align: right; }
```

text-decoration

These are extra graphics the browser places over or near text, such as underlining and strike-through. It also includes the ability to blink text. Don't.

Syntax

```
text-decoration: decoration | none
```

Values

Options available to you are blink | line-through | over-line | underline. Netscape doesn't see the overline value.

Examples

```
B { text-decoration: underline; }
A { text-decoration: none; }
```

text-indent

This sets the size of the indent of the first line of a block of text. You can also use a negative number to outdent the line.

Syntax

```
text-indent: length | percentage
```

Values

The length can be any valid length—see the "Measurement Units" section in Appendix B. The percentage is a percentage of the width of the element.

Examples

```
P { text-indent: 3em; }
P { text-indent: 200%; }
```

text-transform

This attribute governs the capitalization of text. You can capitalize text, turn all the letters uppercase or make them lowercase. Note that this attribute doesn't affect links.

Syntax

```
text-transform: capitalization | none
```

Values

You can use `capitalize` | `uppercase` | `lowercase`. The `capitalize` value transforms the first letter of every word into uppercase, and the other options convert the text into their respective cases.

Examples

```
H2 { text-transform: uppercase; }
B { text-transform: capitalize; }
```

◆ Position Attributes

left

When you position elements, use this attribute to determine how far from the left edge of the browser window the left edge of the element is.

Syntax

```
left: length | percentage | auto
```

Values

You can use any valid length, as described in the "Measurement Units" section in Appendix B. You can use negative values to place elements partially or completely off screen, which is useful for animating elements from off-screen.

Examples

```
H2 { position: relative; left: 3em }
#productShot {position: absolute; top: 50px; left: 300px; }
```

position

This attribute sets whether an element is positionable and what kind of positioning will occur.

Syntax

```
position: position
```

Values

The only two values that work in both browsers are `relative` | `absolute`.

Examples

```
#pants { position: absolute; top: 40px; left: 90px; }
```

top

When you position elements, use this attribute to determine how far from the top edge of the browser window the top edge of the element is.

Syntax

```
top: length | percentage | auto
```

Values

You can use any valid length, as described in the "Measurement Units" section in Appendix B. You can use negative values to place elements partially or completely off-screen, which is useful for animating elements from off-screen.

Examples

```
H2 { position: relative; top: 3em }
#productShot {position: absolute; top: 50px; left: 300px; }
```

visibility

This controls whether positioned elements are visible or not. This reserves space on the page for the element, even if it's rendered invisible. If you don't want space reserved on the page for the element, use the `display` attribute.

Syntax

```
visibility: visibility
```

Values

The only values that work in both browsers are `visible` | `hidden` | `inherit`.

Examples

```
#ecommerce { visibility: hidden; }
```

width

You can control (sort of) the width of your content block with this attribute. We've found it to be most useful in situations where you want your text blocks to be only so wide. However, Netscape and IE treat this attribute pretty differently, so test extensively before taking a page with `width` live.

Syntax

```
width: length | percentage | auto
```

Values

You can use any valid length from the "Measurement Units" section in Appendix B. Using `auto` is the same as not including the attribute at all, and *percentage* is based on the width of the next outermost contained (often the browser window).

Examples

```
#velourTop { width: 350px; }
```

z-index

This attribute sets the stacking order of a positioned element. The default value of all layers is zero, and layers with the same z-index are displayed according to where they appear in the code, so layers that appear last in the code are displayed above layers that appear earlier.

Syntax

```
z-index: integer | auto
```

Values

Any integer will do, even negative ones. Using `auto` is the same thing as using zero.

Examples

```
#superModel { z-index: 4; }
#designer { z-index: 10; }
```

B Miscellaneous Reference

◆ Good Web Resources

As you'd expect, there are many great resources on the Web for learning more about DHTML. Here are some of our favorites:

- DHTML Zone by Macromedia: www.dhtmlzone.com
- ProjectCool: www.projectcool.com
- OpenStudio by Netscape: http://home.netscape.com/computing/webbuilding
- CNET Builder.com: www.builder.com/Authoring/DhtmlSpot/ (lots of good links)

◆ External Stylesheets

It's possible to place your styles and layer declarations and classes in a separate file. If you have several pages that use the same styles, this can be useful, as all the HTML pages can simply reference the same file with the styles in it. We haven't found this feature to be as useful as one would expect, but it's good to know about just in case.

You link to an external stylesheet by including this statement in the <HEAD> of your HTML document:

```
<LINK REL="stylesheet" TYPE="text/css"
HREF="mystyle.css">
```

◆ Positioning Attributes

Here are all the attributes you'll need in order to position your elements exactly where you want them:

Attribute	Description
position	Defines how a layer is to be positioned.
left	The distance from the left edge of a layer to the left edge of that layer's box (the edge of the browser window if the layer isn't nested).
top	The distance from the top edge of a layer to the top edge of that layer's box (the edge of the browser window if the layer isn't nested).
width	The width of a layer (if it's absolutely positioned).
height	The height of a layer (if it's absolutely positioned).
clip	The shape and dimension of the viewable content of a layer.
overflow	How to handle content that exceeds the layer's height/width settings (this can be a little unstable, so test it carefully).
visibility	Whether a layer is visible or not.
z-index	The stacking order of a layer.

◆ Measurement Units

There are many more ways to measure distance with CSS than in regular HTML:

Length Unit	Example	Description
em	2.5em	M-width
ex	2ex	Font x-height
px	37px	Pixel
in	1.25in	Inch
cm	10cm	Centimeter
mm	132mm	Millimeter
pt	14pt	Point (equal to 1/72 of an inch)
pc	1.5pc	Pica (same as 12 points)

You won't use most of these units, but a brief explanation of some of them is in order. An *em* is the width of the lowercase character m. This measurement is used often in typesetting. Also, since the vast majority of computer monitors use 72 dots per inch, pixels and points are the same measurement. The main reason for creating all these measurements is for potential future uses of stylesheets not only for Web pages, but also for printing and other applications.

◆ Colors

Colors can be referred to in several different ways:

By name	color: blue
By hex value	color: #0000FF
By RGB value	color: rgb (0, 0, 255)
By RGB percentage	color: rgb (0%, 0%, 100%)

For the last two, if you enter a value that's over the maximum (above 255 or 100%, respectively), browsers will replace your number with the appropriate maximum.

C JavaScript Reference

This appendix covers only the parts of JavaScript that are available in the 4.x versions of both Netscape and Internet Explorer (IE). We're skipping any objects, properties, or methods that don't work in both browsers. We're also omitting anything referring to VBScript, ActiveX, or LiveConnect.

As a reminder, JavaScript is a Netscape invention that Microsoft copied, altered, and called JScript. Now, a nonplatform-specific scripting language called ECMAScript has been accepted as a common standard. This standard is very similar to JavaScript and is supposed to be implemented in the 5.0 browsers. In this appendix, we note any facet of JavaScript that's accepted by both Netscape and IE, but not by ECMAScript, with a big "NOT ECMA" note.

In case you're wondering, ECMA stands for "European Computer Manufacturers Association," which is an international, Europe-based industry association founded in 1961 and dedicated to the standardization of information and communication systems.

We've divided this reference into several sections:

- *Basic objects (for example,* `Array, Date, Number`*)*
- *Operators (for example,* `+, -, !=`*)*
- *Global functions (for example,* `eval(), toString()`*)*
- *Statements (for example,* `var`*)*

◆ Basic Objects

Array

An *array* is a collection of items of data that have a certain order. Think of drawers in a chest, with each drawer containing a data item. The name of each drawer is called the *index value*. Usually, index values begin at 0 and climb. However, strings can also be used as index values. Index values are placed in square brackets after the array name.

Example

```
ring[0] = "engagement"
ring["tanya"] = "engagement"
```

Both are acceptable. You can create an array with a certain number of items, or drawers, even if some of the drawers are empty, (that is, they have no data in them). Following are the properties and methods associated with arrays (only the cross-browser ones, of course).

length

Counts the number of entries in an array.

Example

```
if (ring.length > 10)
{
    // go broke
}
```

prototype

This is a little complicated. You can assign new properties and methods to an array using prototype. This property is meant to be used to deal with further instances of arrays you've already created earlier in your document.

concat()—NOT ECMA

Allows you to combine several arrays into one. The name of the function comes from *concatenate*, which means "to combine." Neither of the original arrays is affected by this function.

Example

```
var ourFamiliesArray =
myFolksArray.concat(herFolksArray)
```

join()

Joins all of the items in an array in one long string. In between each item is whatever you place between the parentheses in `join()`.

Syntax

```
join(delimiterString)
```

The string in between all the items is called a *delimiter.*

reverse()

Reverses the order of an array and produces a new array with the items in the reverse order.

slice()

Creates an array that's a subset of an array you've already created.

Syntax

```
slice(startIndex, endIndex)
```

The *endIndex* value is optional. If you don't include the *endIndex*, the resulting new array will start at *startIndex* and continue to the end of the original array.

sort()

Sorts the items in your array alphabetically or according to a sorting function that you define.

Example
Alphabetical sort:

```
deskArray.sort()
```

Sort by your own function:

```
function yourSortFunction (x,y)
{
    return (2 * x) / (y - 4)
```

```
}
deskArray.sort(yourSortFunction)
```

Boolean

Boolean objects are pretty simple: Their value is either `true` or `false`.

prototype

Lets you create new methods and properties to future instances of Boolean objects. Honestly, it's hard to imagine a situation where this would actually come in handy, so we'll talk no more of it.

toString()

Returns the object value as a string (that is, `true` or `false`). You'll never need to do this because browsers automatically convert Boolean objects to strings when needed.

valueOf()

Returns an object's value as either `true` or `false`. Again, you don't need to do this if you've already assigned a Boolean value to an object or variable.

Date

Most `Date` objects are snapshots of what time it is, kind of like calling POPCORN on your phone to find out the time. Browsers generally store dates in terms of milliseconds at Coordinated Universal Time (UTC), which is really the same thing as Greenwich Mean Time (GMT). Dates are measured from January 1, 1970 (which is also the year Dan was born). Browsers calculate dates using the time zone setting on the user's computer, so all returned times and dates are local to the user, unless you tell your script to use only UTC or GMT.

Create a new date by:

```
var thisInstant = new Date()
var rightNow = new Date(yy, mm, dd)
```

Other combinations inside the `Date` parentheses are possible.

Let's look at the single property and myriad methods available with the `Date` object.

prototype

If you've been reading along, you've seen this property before. Use it to assign new properties and methods to instances of `Date` objects you've already created in a document. You'll probably never use this.

getDate()

Returns the date within the current month, or in the month you specified when you set the `Date` object.

Example

```
var rightNow = new Date()
var todayDate = rightnow.getDate()
```

getDay()

Returns the number of which day of the week it is. For example, Sunday is 0, Monday is 1, Wednesday is 3.

getFullYear()

Returns all the digits for the year in question. IE will actually let you use years with negative values, but Netscape only goes down to zero.

getHours()

Returns the hour of the day on a 24-hour clock, so `getHours()` would return a time of 1 P.M. as 13.

getMilliseconds()

Returns the number of milliseconds since the seconds value determined by the `Date` object. Values range from 0 to 999.

getMinutes()

Returns the number of minutes since the hours value determined by the `Date` object. Values range from 0 to 59.

getMonth()

Returns the number of the month as determined by the `Date` object. Values range from 0 to 11 (January is 0, March is 2, and so forth).

getSeconds()

Returns the number of seconds since the minutes value determined by the `Date` object. Values range from 0 to 59.

getTime()

Returns the number of milliseconds that have passed since January 1, 1970 to the date specified in the `Date` object.

getTimezoneOffset()

Returns the number of minutes difference between GMT and the time on the user's computer clock. Time zones to the west are positive; time zones to the east are negative. Value is between –720 and 720.

getUTCDate()

Returns the date within the month designated by the `Date` object; in UTC time, it's stored inside the browser.

getUTCDay()

Returns the number of the day of the week. For example, Sunday is 0, Monday is 1, and Wednesday is 3. However, it returns this number in UTC time that's stored inside the browser.

getUTCFullYear()

Returns all the digits for the year in question. IE will actually let you use years with negative values, but Netscape only goes down to zero. However, it returns this number in UTC time that's stored inside the browser.

getUTCHours()

Returns the hour of the day on a 24-hour clock; for example, `getHours()` would return a time of 1 P.M. as 13. However, it returns this number in UTC time that's stored inside the browser.

getUTCMilliseconds()

Returns the number of milliseconds since the seconds value determined by the `Date` object. Values range from 0 to 999. However, it returns this number in UTC time that's stored inside the browser.

getUTCMinutes()

Returns the number of minutes since the hours value determined by the `Date` object. Values range from 0 to 59. However, it returns this number in UTC time that's stored inside the browser.

getUTCMonth()

Returns the number of the month as determined by the `Date` object. Values range from 0 to 11 (January is 0, March is 2, and so forth). However, it returns this number in UTC time that's stored inside the browser.

getUTCSeconds()

Returns the number of seconds since the minutes value determined by the `Date` object. Values range from 0 to 59. However, it returns this number in UTC time that's stored inside the browser.

parse()

Returns the number of milliseconds passed since the date specified in the `DateString`.

```
parse(DateString)
```

setDate()

Sets the day of the month to whatever integer you place between the parentheses. It changes the value of the `Date` object.

setFullYear()

Sets the year to whatever integer you place between the parentheses. It changes the value of the `Date` object.

setHours()

Sets the hour of the day to whatever integer you place between the parentheses. It changes the value of the `Date` object.

setMilliseconds()

Sets the number of milliseconds to whatever integer you place between the parentheses. It changes the value of the `Date` object.

setMinutes()

Sets the minutes past the hour to whatever integer you place between the parentheses. It changes the value of the Date object.

setMonth()

Sets the month of the year to whatever integer you place between the parentheses. It changes the value of the Date object. Values can be between 0 and 11: January is 0, February is 1, and so forth.

setSeconds()

Sets the number of seconds past the latest minute to whatever integer you place between the parentheses. It changes the value of the Date object. Values can be from 0 to 59.

setUTCDate()

Sets the day of the month to whatever integer you place between the parentheses in UTC time. It changes the value of the Date object.

setUTCFullYear()

Sets the year to whatever integer you place between the parentheses. It changes the value of the Date object.

setUTCHours()

Sets the hour of the day to whatever integer you place between the parentheses in UTC time. It changes the value of the Date object.

setUTCMilliseconds()

Sets the number of milliseconds to whatever integer you place between the parentheses in UTC time. It changes the value of the Date object.

setUTCMinutes()

Sets the minutes past the hour to whatever integer you place between the parentheses in UTC time. It changes the value of the Date object.

setUTCMonth()

Sets the month of the year to whatever integer you place between the parentheses in UTC time. It changes the value of the Date object. Values can be between 0 and 11: January is 0, February is 1, and so forth.

setUTCSeconds()

Sets the number of seconds past the latest minute to whatever integer you place between the parentheses in UTC time. It changes the value of the `Date` object. Values range from 0 to 59.

setYear()

Sets the year to whatever integer you place between the parentheses. It changes the value of the `Date` object.

toGMTString()

Returns a string with the GMT value of the `Date` object. This doesn't alter the `Date` object.

toLocaleString()

Returns a string of the date in a format that may be localized for a user in another country.

toString()

Returns the date in a string format.

toUTCString()

Returns a string for the date in UTC time.

UTC()

Returns a numeric approach of the date as stored in the browser (that is, UTC time).

valueOf()

Returns the object's value.

Function

A function is a group of JavaScript statements and commands that can be invoked by either a user's actions on the page or by other scripts on your page. If you'd like further instructions, see our book, *Essential JavaScript for Web Professionals.* You'll love it.

Properties and methods follow.

arguments

Returns an array where each parameter of the function is an element in the array.

caller—NOT ECMA

The caller is the function that called the current function. This property returns a reference to the caller function.

length

Returns the number of parameters defined for a function. For example, `function caterer( a, b, c )` would return a value of 3.

prototype

Use prototype to assign new properties or methods to a future instance of a function.

toString()

Returns the object's value as a string. You don't need this method because browsers automatically do this conversion at appropriate times.

valueOf()

Returns the object's value.

Math

The `Math` object is used only to evaluate expressions or return a value. Make sure you use an uppercase M whenever using this object. Properties and methods of this object follow.

E

Returns Euler's constant (2.718281828...).

Example

```
var nume = Math.E
```

LN2

Returns the natural logarithm of 2.

Example

```
var numln2 = Math.LN2
```

LN10

Returns the natural logarithm of 10.

Example

```
var numln10 = Math.LN10
```

LOG2E

Returns the log base-2 of E.

Example

```
var numlog = Math.LOG2E
```

LOG10E

Returns the log base-10 of E.

Example

```
var numlog = Math.LOG10E
```

PI

Returns the value of p.

Example

```
var pi = Math.PI
```

SQRT1_2

Returns the square root of 1/2.

Example

```
var sqrt_half = Math.SQRT1_2
```

SQRT2

Returns the square root of 2.

Example

```
var sqrt_2 = Math.SQRT2
```

abs()

Returns the absolute value of whatever you place inside the parentheses.

acos()

Returns the arc cosine in radians of whatever you place inside the parentheses.

asin()

Returns the arc sine in radians of whatever you place inside the parentheses.

atan()

Returns the arc tangent in radians of whatever you place inside the parentheses.

atan2()

```
atan2(x,y)
```

Returns the arc tangent in radians of the angle formed by the line on a Cartesian coordinate system from (0,0) to (x,y).

ceil()

Returns the next highest integer that's equal to or greater than whatever you place inside the parentheses.

cos()

Returns the cosine of whatever you place inside the parentheses.

exp()

Returns E raised to the power of whatever you place inside the parentheses.

floor()

Returns the next lowest integer that's equal to or greater than whatever you place inside the parentheses.

log()

Returns the natural logarithm of whatever you place inside the parentheses.

max()

```
max(num1, num2)
```

Returns the greatest value of the two values you place inside the parentheses.

min()

```
min(num1, num2)
```

Returns the lowest value of the values you place inside the parentheses.

pow()

```
pow(num1, num2)
```

Returns the value of the first number raised to the power of the second.

random()

Returns a random number between 0 and 1. To calculate a random number between 0 and n:

```
Math.round(Math.random() * n)
```

round()

Returns an integer based on rounding rules: If the decimal part of the number is less then .5, then the number between the parentheses is converted to the next lowest integer. If the decimal portion is .5 or greater, the number is rounded up.

sin()

Returns the sine of whatever you place inside the parentheses.

sqrt()

Returns the square root of whatever you place inside the parentheses.

tan()

Returns the tangent in radians of whatever you place inside the parentheses.

Number

A NUMBER is an object with any numerical value. It's unlikely you'll ever need to specify something as a NUMBER object because it's usually done automatically. We'll show you the associated properties and methods anyway.

MAX_VALUE

Returns the largest number JavaScript can handle: 1.7976931348623157E+308.

MIN_VALUE

Returns the smallest number JavaScript can handle: 5E-324.

NaN

Stands for "Not a Number." JavaScript will return this result when you try to do something impossible with a number.

NEGATIVE_INFINITY, POSITIVE_INFINITY

Values that are smaller and bigger than MIN_VALUE and MAX_VALUE, respectively. Returns values of -Infinity and Infinity.

prototype

Allows to you assign new properties and methods to a NUMBER object. There are very few reasons to do this—we haven't found any good ones.

toString()

Returns the object's value as a string. For example, 23404 becomes "23404".

valueOf()

Returns the object's value.

Object

An object is a customizable "thing" in your script. It can be almost anything. You can give it certain properties and certain methods. If you create an object and call it `weddingObject`, your wedding object can have different properties, such as `cakeFlavor` and `band`. It can also have methods such as `writeCheck()` and `sendInvitations()`.

Example

```
var weddingObject = new Object(cakeFlavor:"Lemon
Duchess", band:"Red Hot Chili Peppers")
```

prototype

Use this property to assign new properties and methods to future instances of the `OBJECT` object.

Example

```
Object.prototype.numBridesmaids = "five"
var weddingObject = new Object(cakeFlavor:"Lemon
Duchess", band:"Red Hot Chili Peppers")
weddingObject.numBridesmaids = "five"
```

toString()

Returns the object's value as a string.

valueOf()

Returns the object's value.

RegExp—NOT ECMA

The `RegExp` object generates instances of regular expressions and keeps track of regular expressions occurring in the document. A regular expression is what you use to search for a certain string or pattern within a block of text. For example, you can search a string to see if it has a 4-digit number followed by the letter "d." There are many ways to search using regular expression, far more than are detailed here. However, we will show you a summary of term parameters.

Properties of the `RegExp` consist of information about the last operation of any regular expression search that occurred in the document.

input

This is the string that is to be searched using regular expressions.

Example

```
RegExp.input = "Five hundred dollars for a cake?!"
```

lastMatch

Returns the string of the input string that matches the regular expression.

lastParen

Returns the string that matches the last parenthesized subcomponent of the regular expression.

leftContext, rightContext

`leftContext` returns the portion of the input string that's to the left of, but not including, the part of the string that fits the match. Likewise, `rightContext` returns the portion of the input string that's to the right of, but not including, the part of the string that fits the match.

multiline

If a search involves text that's on more than one line (such as a TEXTAREA), `multiline` is set to `true`.

$1, ..., $9

The numbers refer to the parenthesized subcomponents of return results. The order is based on the leftmost parenthesis, starting with 1 on the furthest left-hand side and continuing down.

regular expression

This object is technically an instance of the `RegExp` object. To create a regular expression object, surround your search parameter with forward slashes.

Example

```
var searchParam = /bouquet/
```

The `searchParam` variable can then be used as a parameter in regular expression searches.

These search parameters can also include special metacharacters that stand for patterns instead of individual letters or numbers. These metacharacters are always preceded by a backslash (\). Table C–1 lists a summary of regular expression notation.

TABLE C–1 Regular Expression Search Parameters

Character	Stands for	Example
\b	Word boundary	/\bpa/ matches "party" /ta\b/ matches "fiesta"
\B	Not the boundary of a word	/\Brt/ matches "party" /rt\B/ matches "party"
\d	A number from 0 to 9	/\d\d\d/ matches "420"
\D	A nonnumeral	/\D\D\D/ matches "dog"
\s	Single space	/half\sdrunk/ matches "half drunk"
\S	Single nonspace	/half\Sdrunk/ matches "half-drunk"
\w	Letter, number, or underscore	/1\w\w/ matches "1_A"
\W	Not a letter, number, or underscore	/1\W\W/ matches "1#!"
.	Any character except a newline	/.../ matches "bow"
[...]	Any one of the characters in brackets	/fl[opq]wer/ matches "flower"
[^...]	Not any of the characters in brackets	/fl[^xswd]wer/ matches "flower"
*	Zero or more times	/d*/ matches "" and "23423542328"
?	Zero or one time	/d?/ matches "" and "7"
+	One or more times	/d+/ matches "7" and "23423542328"
{n}	Exactly n time	/d{3}/ matches "123" and "722"
{n, }	N times or more	/d{3, }/ matches "234728742874"

TABLE C-1 Regular Expression Search Parameters (Continued)

Character	Stands for	Example
{n, m}	At least n times, but not more than m times	/d{3,5} matches "2342"
^	Occurs at the beginning of the string or line	/^We/ matches "We need beer."
$	Occurs at the end of a string or line	/$beer./ matches "We need more beer."

Example

```
var myRegExp = /your search pattern/ [g | i | gi]
```

Include the g modifier to allow your expression to work globally. Include the i modifier to ignore case in your search.

global

Returns a Boolean value, specifying whether the expression is set up to work globally.

ignoreCase

Returns a Boolean value, specifying whether the expression is set up to ignore case.

lastIndex

In the string to be searched, returns the index of the character where the next search will begin. For a new search on that string, the value is zero.

source

Returns a string of the characters used to create the regular expression.

compile()

Compiles a regular expression pattern into a genuine regular expression object.

exec()

Performs a search on the string placed between the parentheses.

Example

```
var searchPat = /some search/
var searchResult = myRegExp.exec("Where's my tux?")
```

If the search results in a match, this method returns an array with all of the matches.

test()

Searches the string placed between the parentheses and returns `true` if the search pattern was found, `false` if it wasn't.

String

A String object is a sequence of just about anything you can type on your keyboard, such as "Polonius exits R, pursued by bear" or "32547etr#$%ERT##@R."

String methods come in two categories. The first places HTML tags around strings to make them bold, italic, and so forth. The second category is composed of string manipulation methods. You'll probably use the second category much more frequently than the first.

You don't need to declare a new String object beyond simply declaring a string variable.

Example

```
var bestManDuty = "Bachelor Party"
```

length

Returns the number of characters in a string.

prototype

Allows you to create new properties or methods associated with any new String objects that are created. There's almost never a need to do this.

anchor()—NOT ECMA

Creates a copy of the string with an `<A>` tag around the string, with the NAME attribute being what you've placed inside the parentheses.

big()—NOT ECMA

Creates a copy of the string within a `<BIG>` tag set.

blink()—NOT ECMA

Creates a copy of the string within a `<BLINK>` tag set. But you know better than to do this.

bold()—NOT ECMA

Creates a copy of the string within a `<B>` tag set.

charAt()

```
charAt(position)
```

Returns the character at the position indicated.

charCodeAt()

Returns the decimal Unicode value for the character at the position indicated.

concat()—NOT ECMA

Returns a string that adds the string in the parentheses to the original string.

fixed()—NOT ECMA

Creates a copy of the string within a `<TT>` tag set.

fontcolor()—NOT ECMA

Creates a copy of the string within a `<FONT>` tag set, with a `COLOR` attribute whose value is what's placed between the parentheses.

fontsize()—NOT ECMA

Creates a copy of the string within a `<FONT>` tag set, with a `SIZE` attribute whose value is what's placed between the parentheses.

fromCharCode()—NOT ECMA

```
String.fromCharCode(num1, num2, num3, ... )
```

Returns a string of characters whose Unicode values match the numbers between the parentheses.

indexOf()

```
indexOf(targetString, startPosition)
```

Returns the starting position of the `targetString`, if it's found. If the `targetString` isn't found, a value of –1 is returned. You can also search your string starting at a certain position (`startPosition`).

italics()—NOT ECMA

Creates a copy of the string within an `<I>` tag set.

lastIndexOf()

```
lastIndexOf(subString, startPosition)
```

Returns the starting position of the `targetString`, if it's found. If the `targetString` isn't found, a value of –1 is returned. You can also search your string starting at a certain position (`startPosition`). This method is just like `indexOf()`, but it begins its search from the end of your string and moves toward the beginning.

link()—NOT ECMA

```
link(URL)
```

Creates a copy of the string within an `<A>` tag set, with the `HREF` attribute being what you've placed inside the parentheses.

match()—NOT ECMA

```
match(regularExpression)
```

Returns an array of strings that match the search pattern within your string.

replace()—NOT ECMA

```
replace(regularExpression, replaceString)
```

Returns a new string with the `replaceString` in place of the part of the original string that matched the search pattern in the regular expression.

search()—NOT ECMA

```
search(regularExpression)
```

Returns the position of the first character of the string that matches the search pattern defined in the regular expression. This method is similar to `indexOf()`, but it searches according to a regular expression instead of a small string.

slice()—NOT ECMA

```
slice(startPosition, endPosition)
```

Returns a substring of the current string, starting and ending at the indicated times. The end position is optional; omitting it will cause the substring to end at the end of the original string.

small()—NOT ECMA

Creates a copy of the string within a `<SMALL>` tag set.

split()

```
split(delimiter)
```

Returns an array of the string split into parts. The delimiting character determines where the splits occur. The delimiter is not included in the array.

strike()—NOT ECMA

Creates a copy of the string within a `<STRIKE>` tag set.

sub()—NOT ECMA

Creates a copy of the string within a `<SUB>` tag set.

substr()—NOT ECMA

```
substr(startPosition, length)
```

Returns a substring of the original string starting at `startPosition` and continuing for `length` characters, or until the end of the string, if `length` is omitted.

substring()

```
substring( startPosition, endPosition)
```

Returns a substring of the original string, starting and ending at the values between the parentheses.

sup()—NOT ECMA

Creates a copy of the string within a <SUP> tag set.

toLowerCase(), toUpperCase()

Returns a copy of the string in all lowercase or all uppercase characters.

◆ Operators

+

Adds both numbers and strings.

Example

```
var dressCost = initialCost + alterationsCost
var bandName = "Red Hot " + "Chili Peppers"
```

-

Subtracts one number from another. This operand only works on numbers.

*

Multiplies two numbers.

/

Divides one number by another.

=

A single equal sign is only used to assign a value to a variable or object.

+=

Adds a number or string to the current value.

Example

```
a = 4
a += 5
```

This results in a value of 9 for the variable a. Note it's the same result as

```
a = a + 5.
```

There are many operands that work just like this, as shown in Table C–2.

TABLE C–2 Assignment Operators

Operator	Example	Same Result As
+=	x += y	x = x + y
−=	x −= y	x = x − y
*=	x *= y	x = x * y
/=	x /= y	x = x / y
&=	x &= y	x = x & y
|=	x |= y	x = x | y
%=	x %= y	x = x % y
^=	x ^= y	x = x ^ y
>>>=	x >>>= y	x = x >>> y
<<=	x <<= y	x = x << y
>>=	x >>= y	x = x >> y

&

The bitwise AND operator. The operation compares the binary value of two numbers, and looks at each column of bits. If both columns are a 1, the resulting column in a new number is 1. If not, the resulting new column is 0.

Example

```
var bitMe = 3 & 6
```

The operand looks at the binary values of 3 and 6, which are 0011 and 0110, respectively. The result is 0010, whose decimal equivalent is 2. Thus, the value of `bitMe` is 2. The bitwise, AND, OR, and NOT operators can be combined to create some very powerful and fast conditional statements when used properly. It's unlikely you'll be using them much for DHTML purposes, though.

|

The bitwise OR operator. This functions just like &, the bitwise AND operator, except in reverse: If the column of bits in two numbers is 0, the result is also 0 in the new number. If not, the result is 1 in the new number.

Example

```
var bitMeAgain = 3 | 6
```

This time, 3 and 6 are 0011 and 0110, respectively, and the resulting binary number is 0111, whose decimal equivalent is 7.

<<

The bitwise left-shift operator. This shifts the bits of the first operand by the number of columns specified by the second number. For example, 6 is 0110, and shifting the bits over two columns would result in 11000, which is 24. Note that shifting bits over by one column is the same as doubling the original number. This is a way to multiply a number by powers of 2 in a way that's much, much faster than multiplying.

>>

The bitwise right-shift operator. This shifts the bits of the first operand by the number of columns specified by the second number. For example, 6 is 0110, and shifting the bits over one column would result in 0011, which is 243. Note that shifting bits over by one column is the same as halving the original number. This is a way to divide a number by powers of 2 in a way that's much, much faster than straight division.

~

The bit-wise NOT operator. This inverts the value of each binary digit in a number. For example, 3 is 0011, and running the NOT operator results in 1100. The final decimal equivalent would be –12.

^

The bitwise OR (XOR) operator. When comparing two binary numbers, if either column (but not both) has a 1, then that column in the new number is 1. All other combinations result in 0. For example, 3 ^ 6 would result in 0101, whose decimal equivalent is 5.

>>>

The bitwise zero-fill right-shift operator. This works the same as the right-shift operator (>>), except that >>> fills in the columns to the left with 0s, while >> fills in those columns with 1s.

<, >, <=, >=

The less-than, greater-than, less-than-or-equal-to, and greater-than-or-equal-to operators. These work on both numbers and strings. Nonnumeric comparisons are evaluated according to their Unicode value.

,

The comma operator. This simply separates different values in a script.

Example

```
var caterer1, caterer2, flowerGirl, ringKid
```

That's it.

++

The increment operator. Adds 1 to the current variable.

Example

```
guests++
```

Adds 1 to the variable guests. You can place this operator in front or behind a variable for different effects.

```
var extraGuests, drinkingBuddies
drinkingBuddies = 5
extraGuests = ++drinkingBuddies
```

One is added to `drinkingBuddies` before that total is added to guests. The result is `extraGuests` = 6 and `drinkingBuddies` = 6. If you move the increment operator:

```
extraGuests = drinkingBuddies++
```

the addition to `drinkingBuddies` occurs after `extraGuests` is assigned the value. In this case, `extraGuests` = 5 and `drinkingBuddies` = 6.

`--`

The decrement operator. This works exactly the same as the increment operator `++`, except that 1 is taken away from the value instead of added. Please see the `++` description shown previously for examples.

`==`

The equality operator. This compares two values and sees whether they are equal or not. If they are, a Boolean value of `true` results. If not, `false` is assigned.

`!=`

The inequality operator. Compares two values and if they are not equal, a Boolean value of `true` is assigned. If they are equal, a Boolean value of `false` is assigned.

`%`

The modulus operator. This divides the number on the left by the number on the right and returns the remainder. If there is no remainder, the returned value is 0.

`?:`

```
condition ? action1 : action2
```

The conditional operator. It acts as shorthand for an if/else structure. If the condition is `true`, the first action is executed. If the condition isn't `true`, the second action is executed.

delete

This operator removes a property from an object.

Example

```
delete myWedding.operaMusic
```

Assuming that `operaMusic` had been a previously assigned property of `myWedding`.

◆ Control Statements

break

Stops the current loop in its tracks and starts executing the first statement outside of and below the loop.

continue

Stops the execution of the current iteration of the loop and goes back to the top of the loop.

do/while—NOT ECMA

Executes a series of statements while a certain condition is `true`. Be careful with this one—if you don't provide a way for the condition to eventually prove `false`, an infinite loop results.

Syntax

```
do
{
     statements
}
while (condition)
```

for

Allows you to create a loop, much like `do/while`, but usually specifies a certain number of repetitions before any statements are executed.

Syntax

```
for (initialValue, condition, updateExpression)
{
     statements
}
```

for/in

A variation on the `for` loop that can read property names and values from an object.

Syntax

```
for (variable in objectName)
{
    statements
}
```

if

A conditional statement that provides one possible side route.

Syntax

```
if (condition)
{
    statements
}
```

if/else

A conditional statement that provides a number of alternate paths.

Syntax

```
if (condition)
{
    statements
}
else
{
    statements
}
```

You can also nest another `if` statement in this construct:

```
if (condition1)
{
    statements
}
else if (condition2)
{
    statements
}
else
```

```
{
    statements
}
```

label—NOT ECMA

You can assign a name to a block of code. This is usually used in conjunction with deeply nested loops with lots of breaks and continues. Use of labels lets you control where the breaks and continues occur, and where the control goes when they're executed.

return

Halts execution of the current function. You can also return a value, if you want.

Example

```
return
```

or

```
return photographerName
```

switch/case—NOT ECMA

Provides a shortcut for long if/else statements.

Syntax

```
switch (expression)
{
    case label1:
        statements
        break
    case label1:
        statements
        break
    ...
    default:
        statements
}
```

The default case is optional.

while

Executes statements in a loop while a certain condition is `true`. Like the `do`/`while` structure, this can result in an infinite loop if you don't provide a way for the condition to eventually be `false`.

Syntax

```
while (expression)
{
    statements
}
```

with

This adds the name of an object to every statement inside the `with` block. You'd use this to make your code shorter and a little more readable.

Syntax

```
with (objectName)
{
    statements
}
```

◆ Global Functions

escape

```
escape(URL)
```

Returns a string encoded for use in a URL. For instance, a space will be converted to %20. Note that plus symbols are not converted, because they're often used as a part of the URL. If you need to have plus signs encoded as well, add a ", 1" after the URL.

eval()

We discussed this function when we talked about cross-browser DHTML. It takes a string and executes that string as if it were a JavaScript statement. Read Chapter 3 for a full description of this function.

isFinite()

Evaluates the expression between the parentheses and returns a Boolean value of `true` if the expression falls between `MAX_VALUE` and `MIN_VALUE`.

isNaN()

Evaluates the expression between the parentheses and returns a Boolean value of `true` if the expression is not a number.

parseInt()

Parses the initial integers out of a string. However, if your string begins with a letter, this method will return `NaN`.

parseFloat()

Parses the initial integers or floating-point numbers out of the string placed between the parentheses. If the string doesn't begin with a number, only `NaN` will be returned.

toString()—NOT ECMA

```
numberVariable.toString(base)
```

Returns a string version of the `numberVariable`, after converting it to the base described between the parentheses.

unescape()

Returns a decoded version of a URL (the opposite of `escape()`). For example, all "%20"s in the URL will be converted to single whitespaces.

◆ Statements

//, / ... */*

These are comment statements. Comments are nonexecuted statements that exist for the sole purpose of explaining the surrounding code.

The `//` is a single-line comment statement:

```
// the code below doesn't work
```

The `/* ... */` can be a single- or multiline comment:

```
/*
    Here's where I set the array.
    more comments
    more comments
*/
```

this

Use this word to refer to the current object, instead of having to use the object's full name.

var

Allows to you declare a variable. Using this statement is optional.

D Cross-Browser DOM Reference

Browsers break up Web pages into little distinct bits called objects. Since these objects are in the Web page document, they're called document objects. When we use DHTML to make elements for our Web pages, we use JavaScript to affect these objects. Browsers organize these objects and refer to them using the Document Object Model, or DOM. Internet Explorer (IE) and Netscape Navigator are different browsers, so they break up Web pages in different ways—they have different DOMs. There's some overlap to their DOMs (you refer to images in both browsers with images), but there are many differences. This makes life difficult for Web developers, because we try to write a single script that works in both browsers. Often, we're forced to write two scripts that deal with the different DOMs.

What we've done in this appendix is list all the objects that are the same for both IE and Navigator, along with any event handlers that go with the object (for example, onmouseover with AREA). If an object is available for use with Netscape and not for IE, we don't list it. If an object is available for IE but not Netscape, it's not listed here. IE version 4.0 utilizes many more document objects than Netscape version 4.0—listing all the objects available to just IE or Navigator is beyond the scope of this book.

We've listed everything in alphabetical order. Good hunting!

◆ A

We mean A as in <A>, the anchor tag. You can refer to an anchor
in two ways.

Object Reference

```
document.links[n]
document.anchors[n]
```

Where n stands for which number the <A> is if all the anchor
tags in the document are given a number, starting with 0 for
the first one.

hash

The hash of a URL is the part that follows the # symbol. It usually refers to a place in a document where you've created an
<A NAME="foo">.

Example

```
document.links[3].hash = "authorBio"
```

host

The combination of the hostname (for example, www.wire-
man.com) and the port (if any) of the destination server to which
the link is pointing. If no port is listed, the default port of 80 is
assumed. Always separate the hostname and the port number
with a colon, as in a URL.

Example

```
document.links[3].host = "www.wire-man.com:80"
```

hostname

The name of the server to which the link is pointing; for example,
www.wire-man.com or www.etail.com.

Example

```
document.links[2].hostname = "www.paletteman.com"
```

href

The fully described destination of the link, as coded in that link's
HREF statement.

Example

```
document.links[5].href = "http://www.wire-man.com"
```

name

The value of the NAME attribute in the `<A>` tag. You can also give anchors names.

Example

```
document.anchors[3].name = "authorBio"
```

pathname

The part of the URL that doesn't have the server name or port number in it.

Example

```
document.links[1].pathname = "/clients/reallybig/
biggest.html"
```

port

The port number of the server to which the link is pointing. This is usually assumed to be 80, the default port for Web connections.

Example

```
document.links['authorBio'].port = "80"
```

protocol

The protocol assigned for the link to the destination server. This protocol is usually `"http:"`, `"ftp:"`, `"file:"`, `"mailto:"`, or `"https:"`.

Example

```
document.authorBio.protocol = "http:"
```

search

The part of a URL that's after the ? character. Using ? is a way to transfer information besides just the URL. You've seen these URLs if you've ever used a search engine like Yahoo!.

Example

```
document.links[7].search =
"?name=Bob&platform=Mac&edt=032874djhs"
```

target

The name of the frame or window in which the new page will be displayed.

Example

```
document.links[3].target = "_top"
document. links [4].target = "mainNavFrame"
```

◆ Anchors

You've seen these before. Anchors are those `<A>` tags that use NAME, which separates them from links, which use HREF. Like most objects, you can reference them by the order in which they were loaded on the page, or by their name.

Object Reference

```
document.anchors[n]
document.anchors['anchorName']
```

length

The length property describes how many anchors there are in the document. If you have three tags in your document that look like `<A NAME="someThing">`, then you'll be returned a value of 3.

Example

```
var howManyAnchors = document.anchors.length
```

◆ Applets

This element refers to any `<APPLET>` tags you have in your document. Refer to them by number.

Object Reference

```
document.applet[n]
```

length

The length property describes how many applets there are in the document. If you have three tags in your document that look like `<APPLET ...>`, then you'll be returned a value of 3.

Example

```
var howManyApplets = document.applets.length
```

◆ Area

Refers to any <AREA> tags in your document. They usually show up nested inside a <MAP> tagset. They're dealt with in almost exactly the same way as regular links.

Event Handlers

You can use these event handlers when dealing with AREA objects:

- onmouseout
- onmouseover

hash

The hash of a URL is the part that follows the # symbol. It usually refers to a place in a document where you've created an <A NAME="foo">.

Example

```
document.links[3].hash = "authorBio"
```

host

The combination of the hostname (for example, www.wire-man.com) and the port (if any) of the destination server to which the link is pointing. If no port is listed, the default port of 80 is assumed. Always separate the hostname and the port number with a colon, as in a URL.

Example

```
document.links[3].host = "www.wire-man.com:80"
```

hostname

The name of the server to which the link is pointing; for example, www.wire-man.com or www.etail.com.

Example

```
document.links[2].hostname = "www.paletteman.com"
```

href

The fully described destination of the link, as coded in that link's HREF statement.

Example

```
document.links[5].href = "http://www.wire-man.com"
```

name

The value of the NAME attribute in the <A> tag. You can also give anchors names.

Example

```
document.anchors[3].name = "authorBio"
```

pathname

The part of the URL that doesn't have the server name or port number in it.

Example

```
document.links[1].pathname = "/clients/reallybig/
biggest.html"
```

port

The port number of the server to which the link is pointing. This is usually assumed to be 80, the default port for Web connections.

Example

```
document.links['authorBio'].port = "80"
```

protocol

The protocol assigned for the link to the destination server. This protocol is usually "http:", "ftp:", "file:", "mailto:", or "https:".

Example

```
document.authorBio.protocol = "http:"
```

search

The part of a URL that's after the ? character. Using ? is a way to transfer information besides just the URL. You've seen these URLs if you've ever used a search engine like Yahoo!.

Example

```
document.links[7].search =
"?name=Bob&platform=Mac&edt=032874djhs"
```

target

The name of the frame or window in which the new page will be displayed.

Example

```
document.links[3].target = "_top"
document.links[4].target = "mainNavFrame"
```

◆ Button

Refers to a BUTTON element, usually seen in an <INPUT TYPE="button"> tag. It's referred to as either an element in a form, or by its name.

Object Reference

```
document.forms[n].elements[n]
document.formName.elementName
```

Event Handlers

You can use these event handlers when dealing with BUTTON objects:

- onclick
- onmousedown
- onmouseup

form

Refers to any FORM objects you have in your document. This is usually used in conjunction with a call to an event handler in the HTML.

Example

```
<INPUT TYPE="button"
    VALUE="Click to Check Form"
    onClick="errorCheck(this.form)">
```

name

The value of the NAME attribute in the BUTTON tag. You can also give elements names by scripting them.

Examples

```
if (document.quizForm.bigButton.name == "clickThis") { ... }
document.quizForm.bigButton.name = "boyHowdy"
```

type

Refers to the value of the TYPE attribute of an INPUT element. Any of the following values are valid:

```
button
checkbox
file
hidden
image
password
radio
reset
select-multiple
select-one
submit
text
textarea
```

Example

```
if (document.orderForm.addressBox.type == "text") { ... }
```

value

This is text that appears on the button: the VALUE attribute.

Example

```
document.theForm.theButton.value = "Click me you fool."
```

◆ Checkbox

This refers to the CHECKBOX elements in a form. It's referred to in the same way as are all FORM elements.

Object Reference

```
document.formName.elementName
document.forms[n].elements[n]
```

checked

This returns a Boolean value of whether or not that element is checked.

Example

```
if (document.forms[2].happyCheckbox.checked) { ... }
```

defaultChecked

Returns whether the element is set to be checked when the page loads.

Example

```
if (document.weddingForm.foundMinister.defaultChecked) { ... }
```

form

Refers to any FORM objects you have in your document. This is usually used in conjunction with a call to an event handler in the HTML.

Example

```
<INPUT TYPE="checkbox" NAME="foundMinister"
    onClick="errorCheck(this.form)">
```

name

The value of the NAME attribute in the checkbox tag. You can also give elements names by scripting them.

Example

```
document.quizForm.checkThis.name == "clickThis"
```

type

Refers to the value of the TYPE attribute of an INPUT element. Any of the following values are valid:

```
button
checkbox
file
hidden
image
password
radio
reset
select-multiple
```

```
select-one
submit
text
textarea
```

Example

```
if (document.orderForm.addressBox.type == "text") { ... }
```

◆ Document

The DOCUMENT object is the content within a window or a frame, along with all the information from the HEAD portion of the document.

Object Reference

```
document
window.document
```

alinkColor

The color of a link as it's being clicked.

Example

```
document.alinkColor = "#FFCC33"
```

bgColor

The background color of a document.

Example

```
document.bgColor = "#003399"
```

cookie

You can read and write cookies that follow a user's browser throughout a site. A cookie typically consists of a number of name-value pairs. When you read these pairs from a cookie, they end up being a comma-delimited list: name1=value1;name2=value2;...;nameX=valueX. It's up to your code to parse out the data in this list.

The next example shows you how to write a cookie.

Example

```
document.cookie = "band=ChiliPeppers;
cakeFlavor=LemonDuchess; guests=100"
```

domain

The name of the server that served up the document. For example, if you're looking at a page at http://www.wire-man.com/clients/big-Client.html, the domain would be `wire-man.com`. Setting this property can allow documents from different servers to trade information with each other, since JavaScript doesn't let pages from different domains talk to each other for security reasons.

Example

```
document.domain = "judylepire.com"
```

fgColor

This refers to the foreground color, which is really the text color of the document.

Example

```
document.fgColor = "#336699"
```

lastModified

The date the document was last modified. It comes in the form of a string.

Example

```
var now = new Date()
if (document.lastModified < now) {…}
```

linkColor

The color of a link that points to a document the user hasn't seen yet.

Example

```
document.linkColor = "#000000"
```

location

The URL of the current document. This isn't used much anymore—use `location.href` to move to another document.

Example

```
document.location = "wedding/ceremony/music.html"
```

referrer

The URL of the page that linked to the current page, if the current page was arrived at via a link.

Example

```
if (document.referrer == "http://www.yahoo.com") {…}
```

title

Refers to the TITLE property of the current document, as defined in the HEAD portion of the document.

Example

```
document.title = "Palette Man"
```

URL

The URL of the current document, much the same as the location property. It's the same thing as location.href.

Example

```
document.URL = "http://www.compumotor.com"
```

vlinkColor

The color of a link that points to a document the user's already been to.

Example

```
document.vlinkColor = "#333333"
```

clear()

This is buggy in older browsers. It clears content from the current window. You usually don't need to invoke this method.

Example

```
document.clear()
```

---

close()

This closes the document writing stream to a window or frame. If you're writing to a document using write() or writeln(), you must use close() to make sure the content appears.

Example

```
document.close()
```

open()

Opens an "output stream" to the current document, which means that it opens the door for you to be able to write to the document using write() or writeln(). In fact, you can use document.write() or document.writeln() to automatically take care of this for you.

Syntax

```
open("MIMEtype")
```

Example

```
open("text/html", "replace")
```

The only MIME type allowed by both browsers is "text/html". The "replace" option replaces the current document's entry with the new document about to be written.

write(), writeln()

If you use these methods as the page is loading, you can dynamically create content on the page. The only difference between the two methods is that writeln() adds a carriage return at the end of the line. The carriage return doesn't appear in the browser window, but it does appear in the source code, which can improve readability.

Syntax

```
document.write("string")
document.writeln("string")
```

anchors[]

This is an array of all the anchors in your document; that is, all the <A> tags that have a NAME attribute (they can be links as well). You can refer to any of these anchors by number or by name. The browser determines the number: Each anchor is given a number as it appears in the code, starting with 0 for the first one. The name is determined by the value of the NAME attribute.

applets[]

This is an array of all the Java applets in your document; that is, all the <APPLET> tags. Refer to any of these applets by number. The browser determines the number: Each anchor is given a number as it appears in the code, starting with 0 for the first applet.

forms[]

This is an array of all the forms in your document; that is, all the <FORM> tags. You can refer to any of these forms by number or by name. The browser determines the number: Each form is given a number as it appears in the code, starting with 0 for the first one. The name is determined by the value of the NAME attribute.

images[]

This is an array of all the images in your document; that is, all the <IMG> tags. You can refer to any of these images by number or by name. The browser determines the number: Each image is given a number as it appears in the code, starting with 0 for the first one. The name is determined by the value of the NAME attribute.

links[]

This is an array of all the links in your document; that is, all the <A> tags that have a HREF attribute, as well as any <AREA> tags. You can refer to any of these links by number. The browser determines the number: Each link is given a number as it appears in the code, starting with 0 for the first link.

◆ Elements[]

This is an array of all the elements inside a form in your document. Each form gets its own array of elements. Elements can be referred to by number or by name. The browser determines the number: Each form is given a number as it appears in the code, starting with 0 for the first one. The name is determined by the value of the NAME attribute.

Object Reference

```
document.forms[n].elements[n]
document.formName.elementName
```

◆ Embeds

Refers to any EMBED elements in your document; that is, all the <EMBED> tags.

Object Reference

```
document.embeds
```

length

The length property describes how many embedded elements are in the document.

◆ Event

An event occurs when the user does something on the screen, like clicking a button or moving a mouse over an image. Unfortunately, Netscape and Internet Explorer refer to these events in different ways.

Object Reference

```
// Netscape
eventObj

// IE
window.event
```

screenX, screenY

Returns the x- and y-coordinates. These coordinates are based on the whole video screen, not the edge of the browser window.

Example

```
// Netscape
var xCoord = evtObj.screenX

// IE
var yCoord = window.event.screenY
```

type

The type of the current event, without the on prefix.

Example

```
// Netscape
if (evtObj.type == "mouseover") { ... }

// IE
if (window.event.type == "focus") { ... }
```

◆ fileUpload

Refers to the tag <INPUT TYPE= "file">. This is the tag that results in a text field with a Browse... button. It's referred to in the same way as other FORM elements.

Object Reference

```
document.forms[n].elements[n]
document.formName.elementName
```

Event Handlers

- onblur
- onfocus
- onselect

form

Refers to any FORM objects you have in your document. This is usually used in conjunction with a call to an event handler in the HTML.

Example

```
<INPUT TYPE="button"
    VALUE="Click to Check Form"
    onClick="errorCheck(this.form)">
```

name

The value of the NAME attribute in the <INPUT> tag. You can also give elements names.

Example

```
document.forms[2].elements[4].name = "uploadMusicians"
```

type

Refers to the value of the TYPE attribute of an INPUT element. Any of the following values are valid:

```
button
checkbox
file
hidden
image
password
radio
reset
select-multiple
select-one
submit
text
textarea
```

Example

```
if (document.orderForm.addressBox.type == "text") { ... }
```

value

For the fileUpload object, the value is the URL for the file that the user points to after clicking the Browse... button.

select()

Selects all the text displayed in the element's textbox.

◆ Form

Refers to any FORM objects in the document. Forms can be referred to in several ways.

Object Reference

```
document.forms[2]
document.formName
document.forms['formName']
```

Event Handlers

- onreset
- onsubmit

action

The URL to which the form data is being sent.

Example

```
document.uploadButton.action = "http://
www.abigcompany.com/forms.cgi"
```

encoding

Sets the MIME type for the data that's in the file to be uploaded.

Example

```
document.upload.encoding = "text/html"
```

length

The number of elements in the form.

Example

```
var totalElements = document.longForm.length
```

method

Determines how the form data is sent. You have two options: get and post. The get option appends the data to the URL, while post sends the data as a transaction message body.

Example

```
document.orderForm.method = "post"
```

name

The name of the form.

Example

```
document.forms[2].name = "orderForm"
```

target

The name of the window or frame that is to receive content after the form is submitted.

Example

```
document.forms[4].target = "_parent"
```

reset()

Does the same thing as a user clicking an <INPUT TYPE="reset"> button.

Example

```
document.shortForm.reset()
```

submit()

Does the same thing as a user clicking an <INPUT TYPE="submit"> button.

Example

```
document.shortForm.submit()
```

elements[]

This is an array of all the elements inside a form in your document. Each form gets its own array of elements. Elements can be referred to by number or by name. The browser determines the number: Each form is given a number as it appears in the code, starting with 0 for the first one. The name is determined by the value of the NAME attribute.

◆ Forms[]

An array of all the forms in the document.

Object Reference

```
document.forms[n]
```

length

The number of elements in the specified form.

Example

```
document.forms[3].length
```

◆ Frames[]

Refers to any frames in the current document.

Object Reference

```
frames[n]
```

length

Returns the number of frames in a window.

◆ Hidden

Refers to any `<INPUT type="hidden">` elements in your document. It's referred to in the same way as other form elements.

Object Reference

```
document.forms[n].elements[n]
document.formName.elementName
```

form

Refers to any `FORM` objects you have in your document. This is usually used in conjunction with a call to an event handler in the HTML.

Example

```
<INPUT TYPE="button"
       VALUE="Click to Check Form"
       onClick="errorCheck(this.form)">
```

name

The value of the `NAME` attribute in the `<INPUT>` tag. You can also give elements names.

Example

```
document.forms[2].elements[4].name = "uploadMusicians"
```

type

Refers to the value of the TYPE attribute of an INPUT element. Any of the following values are valid:

```
button
checkbox
file
hidden
image
password
radio
reset
select-multiple
select-one
submit
text
textarea
```

Example

```
if (document.orderForm.addressBox.type == "text") { … }
```

value

For the fileUpload object, the value is the URL for the file that the user points to after clicking the Browse... button.

◆ History

The HISTORY object keeps track of all the URLs a user's browser visits. This history list is off-limits to simple JavaScript and requires signed scripts and the user's approval. We won't go into signed scripts here.

length

The number of items in the history list.

Example

```
numVisits = history.length()
```

back()

The same as pressing the Back button on the browser.

Example

```
history.back()
```

forward()

The same as pressing the Forward button on the browser.

◆ Images[]

This is an array of all the images inside a form in your document. Images can be referred to by number or by name. The browser determines the number: Each image is given a number as it appears in the code, starting with 0 for the first one. The name is determined by the value of the NAME attribute.

Object Reference

```
document.images[n]
document.imageName
document.images['imageName']
```

Event Handlers

* onabort
* onerror
* onload

length

The number of images in the document.

Example

```
var totalImages = document.images.length
```

border

Determines the thickness of the border around an image. This is read-only in Navigator.

height, width

Returns the height and width in pixels of the specified image.

Example

```
var imageSize = document.images[4].height
```

hspace, vspace

Returns the hspace and vspace of the specified image.

Example

```
var imageSpace = document.images[4].hspace
```

lowsrc

The URL of an image that's the same dimension as the final image to download quickly and give the user something to look at while the larger file sized image downloads.

Example

```
document.images[3].lowsrc = "http://www.somecompany.com/
images/sidenav_low.gif"
```

name

The value of the NAME attribute in the <IMG> tag. You can also give images names.

Example

```
document.images[2].name = "side_navigation"
```

◆ Links[]

Refers to all the <A> elements that have HREF.

length

Returns the number of links in the document.

◆ Location

Each window and frame has its own LOCATION object, which is the URL of the content in that window or frame.

Object Reference

```
window.location
```

The `window.` is optional.

hash

The `hash` of a URL is the part that follows the # symbol. It usually refers to a place in a document where you've created an `<A NAME="foo">`.

Example

```
location.hash = "authorBio"
```

host

The combination of the hostname (for example, www.wire-man.com) and the port (if any) of the destination server to which the link is pointing. If no port is listed, the default port of 80 is assumed. Always separate the hostname and the port number with a colon, as in a URL.

Example

```
location.host = "www.wire-man.com:80"
```

hostname

The name of the server; for example, www.wire-man.com or www.compumotor.com.

Example

```
location.hostname = "www.paletteman.com"
```

href

The fully described URL of the content of the current document. Use this property to point the browser to a new page.

Example

```
location.href = "http://www.wire-man.com"
```

pathname

The part of the current document's URL that doesn't have the server name or port number in it.

Example

```
location.pathname = "/clients/reallybig/biggest.html"
```

port

The port number of the server to which the link is pointing. This is usually assumed to be 80, the default port for Web connections.

Example

```
location.port = "80"
```

protocol

The protocol assigned for the link to the destination server. This protocol is usually `"http:"`, `"ftp:"`, `"file:"`, `"mailto:"`, or `"https:"`.

Example

```
location.protocol = "http:"
```

search

The part of a URL that's after the ? character. Using ? in a URL is a way to send extra information to a Web server beyond just which Web page should be shown. You've seen URLs that use this technique if you've ever used a search engine like Yahoo!.

Example

```
location.search =
"?name=Bob&platform=Mac&edt=032874djhs"
```

reload()

Just like pressing the Reload button on a browser.

replace()

Loads a new document into the browser, and the new URL replaces the current document's entry in the browser's history list. After using this method, pressing the Back button won't return the user to the page he or she was just looking at.

◆ Navigator

Essentially, this refers to which browser the user is using.

appCodeName

This returns "Mozilla," no matter which browser you're using.

appName

Returns the name of the browser. For Netscape and IE, the returned values are "Netscape" and "Microsoft Internet Explorer," respectively.

appVersion

Returns the version number of the browser, along with which operating system the user is using.

Examples of Returned Values

Netscape:

```
4.02 (Macintosh; I; PPC)
4.04 [en] (Win95; I)
```

IE:

```
4.0 (compatible; MSIE 4.0; Macintosh; I; PPC)
4.0 (compatible; MSIE 4.0; Windows 95)
```

platform

Returns the name of the operating system or platform of the browser.

Examples of Returned Values

```
Win32
MacPPC
```

userAgent

Returns full information about the browser, including name, browser version, and operating system.

javaEnabled()

Returns a Boolean value as to whether or not Java is turned on in the browser.

◆ Option

Refers to the OPTION elements in the document, the ones found inside a <SELECT> tagset.

Object Reference

```
document.forms[n].elements[n].options[n]
document.formName.elementName.options[n]
```

defaultSelected

Returns whether the specified OPTION has a SELECTED attribute in it.

index

Returns the index of the specified OPTION. Since you have to use the index in order to specify an option, there's not much point in using this property.

length

Returns the number of options in a specified SELECT element.

selected

Returns a Boolean value of true if the user has selected the specified option.

Example

```
if (document.orderForm.productList.options[2].selected) {…}
```

text

Refers to the text after the OPTION tag and what appears in the SELECT box.

value

Refers to the value of the VALUE attribute in the OPTION tag; for example, `<OPTION VALUE="4 items">4`.

◆ Password

Refers to any `<INPUT type="password">` elements in your document. It's referred to in the same way as other FORM elements.

Object Reference

```
document.forms[n].elements[n]
document.formName.elementName
```

defaultValue

The default text for the specified PASSWORD element, established by its VALUE attribute.

form

Refers to any FORM objects you have in your document. This is usually used in conjunction with a call to an event handler in the HTML.

Example

```
<INPUT TYPE="button"
    VALUE="Click to Check Form"
    onClick="errorCheck(this.form)">
```

name

The value of the NAME attribute in the BUTTON tag. You can also give elements names by scripting them.

Example

```
if (document.quizForm.bigButton.name == "clickThis) { ... }
document.quizForm.bigButton.name = "boyHowdy"
```

type

Refers to the value of the TYPE attribute of an INPUT element. Any of the following values are valid:

```
button
checkbox
file
hidden
image
password
radio
reset
select-multiple
select-one
submit
text
textarea
```

Example

```
if (document.orderForm.addressBox.type == "text") { … }
```

value

This is text that appears on the button: the VALUE attribute.

blur()

Removes the focus from the password text box.

focus()

Places focus on the specified password text box.

select()

Selects all the text in the specified password text box.

◆ Radio

Event Handlers

- onclick
- onmousedown
- onmouseup

This refers to the RADIO elements in a form. It's referred to in the same way as all other FORM elements.

Object Reference

```
document.formName.elementName
document.forms[n].elements[n]
```

checked

This returns a Boolean value of whether or not that element is checked.

Example

```
if (document.forms[2].happyRadio.radio) { ... }
```

defaultChecked

Returns whether the element is set to be selected when the page loads.

Example

```
if (document.weddingForm.foundMinister.defaultChecked) { ... }
```

form

Refers to any FORM objects you have in your document. This is usually used in conjunction with a call to an event handler in the HTML.

Example

```
<INPUT TYPE="radio" NAME="foundMinister"
    onClick="errorCheck(this.form)">
```

name

The value of the NAME attribute in the radio tag. You can also give elements names by scripting them.

Example

```
document.quizForm.checkThis.name == "clickThis"
```

type

Refers to the value of the TYPE attribute of an INPUT element. Any of the following values are valid:

```
button
checkbox
file
hidden
image
```

```
password
radio
reset
select-multiple
select-one
submit
text
textarea
```

Example

```
if (document.orderForm.addressBox.type == "text") { … }
```

◆ Reset

Refers to the RESET element, which appears in HTML as <INPUT TYPE="reset">. Refer to this element in the same way as other FORM elements.

Object Reference

```
document.formName.elementName
document.forms[n].elements[n]
```

form

Refers to any FORM objects you have in your document. This is usually used in conjunction with a call to an event handler in the HTML.

Example

```
<INPUT TYPE="radio" NAME="foundMinister"
        onClick="errorCheck(this.form)">
```

name

The value of the NAME attribute in the radio tag. You can also give elements names by scripting them.

Example

```
document.quizForm.checkThis.name == "clickThis"
```

type

Refers to the value of the TYPE attribute of an INPUT element. Any of the following values are valid:

```
button
checkbox
file
hidden
image
password
radio
reset
select-multiple
select-one
submit
text
textarea
```

Example

```
if (document.orderForm.addressBox.type == "text") { … }
```

◆ Screen

This refers to the whole video screen—the whole monitor.

availHeight, availWidth

This measures how many pixels are visible in the user's monitor, not including the 24-pixel task bar at the bottom of Windows systems, or the 20-pixel menu bar at the top of Macintosh systems.

colorDepth

This measures how many bits per pixel are used to display color. One-bit color is black and white, while 8-bit color is 256 colors, and 24-bit color is millions of colors.

height, width

This measures the same video monitor height and width in pixels as availHeight, availWidth, but includes the task bar on Windows systems and the top menu bar on a Macintosh.

◆ Select

Refers to the SELECT element. You refer to this element the same way as all other FORM elements.

Object Reference

```
document.formName.elementName
document.forms[n].elements[n]
```

form

Refers to any FORM objects you have in your document. This is usually used in conjunction with a call to an event handler in the HTML.

Example

```
<INPUT TYPE="radio" NAME="foundMinister"
    onClick="errorCheck(this.form)">
```

length

The number of OPTION elements inside the SELECT element.

name

The value of the NAME attribute in the SELECT tag. You can also give this element a name by scripting it directly.

selectedIndex

Returns the index of a user-selected item. If the SELECT element is set up for multiple selections, the index of the first selected item is returned.

type

Refers to the value of the TYPE attribute of an INPUT element. Any of the following values are valid:

```
button
checkbox
file
hidden
image
password
radio
reset
select-multiple
select-one
submit
text
textarea
```

Example

```
if (document.orderForm.addressBox.type == "text") { … }
```

◆ Submit

Refers to all the Submit buttons in the document (even though there's usually only one). Refer to this element in the same way as most other FORM elements.

Object Reference

```
document.formName.elementName
document.forms[n].elements[n]
```

form

Refers to any FORM objects you have in your document. This is usually used in conjunction with a call to an event handler in the HTML.

Example

```
<INPUT TYPE="radio" NAME="foundMinister"
    onClick="errorCheck(this.form)">
```

name

The value of the NAME attribute in the SELECT tag. You can also give this element a name by scripting it directly.

selectedIndex

Returns the index of a user-selected item. If the SELECT element is set up for multiple selections, the index of the first selected item is returned.

type

Refers to the value of the TYPE attribute of an INPUT element. Any of the following values are valid:

```
button
checkbox
file
hidden
image
password
```

```
radio
reset
select-multiple
select-one
submit
text
textarea
```

Example

```
if (document.orderForm.addressBox.type == "text") { … }
```

value

Refers to the VALUE attribute.

◆ Text

Refers to the TEXT element in the document: <INPUT TYPE="text">.
Refer to this element in the same way as other FORM elements.

Object Reference

```
document.formName.elementName
document.forms[n].elements[n]
```

Event Handlers

- onblur
- onchange
- onfocus
- onkeydown
- onkeypress
- onkeyup
- onselect

defaultValue

The default value for the text box that's established by the VALUE attribute.

form

Refers to any FORM objects you have in your document. This is usually used in conjunction with a call to an event handler in the HTML.

Example

```
<INPUT TYPE="radio" NAME="foundMinister"
    onClick="errorCheck(this.form)">
```

name

The value of the NAME attribute in the SELECT tag. You can also give this element a name by scripting it directly.

type

Refers to the value of the TYPE attribute of an INPUT element. Any of the following values are valid:

```
button
checkbox
file
hidden
image
password
radio
reset
select-multiple
select-one
submit
text
textarea
```

Example

```
if (document.orderForm.addressBox.type == "text") { ... }
```

value

Refers to the VALUE attribute.

blur()

Removes the focus from the password text box.

focus()

Places focus on the specified password text box.

select()

Selects all the text in the specified password text box.

◆ Textarea

Refers to the TEXTAREA element in the document: <TEXTAREA>. Refer to this element in the same way as other FORM elements.

Object Reference

```
document.formName.elementName
document.forms[n].elements[n]
```

defaultValue

The default text in the text area, as defined by the text placed between <TEXTAREA> and </TEXTAREA>.

form

Refers to any FORM objects you have in your document. This is usually used in conjunction with a call to an event handler in the HTML.

Example

```
<TEXTAREA NAME="suggestion"
onBlur="errorCheck(this.form)">
```

name

The value of the NAME attribute in the TEXTAREA tag. You can also give this element a name by scripting it directly.

value

Refers to the VALUE attribute.

blur()

Removes the focus from the text area.

focus()

Places focus on the specified text area.

select()

Selects all the text in the specified text area.

◆ Window

The WINDOW object can be a frame, a full browser window, or a new window the browser opens. Using the WINDOW object can be very useful when you want information to flow from one window to another.

closed

Returns a Boolean value describing whether the specified window has been closed or not. A value of true means the window is closed and none of its objects or element can be accessed.

defaultStatus

The default status message is what appears in the browser's status bar when no document is being loaded. Use the status property to temporarily change the status message (usually done in conjunction with mouseovers).

history

The HISTORY object keeps track of all the URLs a user's browser visits. This history list is off-limits to simple JavaScript and requires signed scripts and the user's approval. We won't go into signed scripts here.

location

The URL of the current document. This isn't used much anymore—use location.href to move to another document.

Example

```
window.document.location = "wedding/ceremony/music.html"
```

name

The name associated with a certain window. This name can be set for a frame with <FRAME NAME="..."> and for a new window with the open() method. The main browser window doesn't have a name.

Syntax

```
windowReference.name
```

opener

Refers to the window or frame that used an `open()` method to open the specified window. This is a way to reference another window and get information from that window about, for example, data a user has entered into a form, or images a user has clicked on.

Syntax

```
opener.document.objectReference
```

parent

Refers to the window that contains the frameset of which the current window is a part.

Syntax

```
parent.windowReference.document.objectReference
```

self

Refers to the current window. It's not necessary to use this, as you can use `window` to mean the same thing, but sometimes it can improve readability in your scripts if they're complicated.

status

Refers to the text in the status bar of the browser. Generally, we don't recommend using this method: Few users look at the status bar, and if information is important enough to be displayed, it should be on the screen, not hidden at the bottom of the browser.

Syntax

```
window.status = "string"
```

top

Refers to the window in the topmost position. This is often used by frames to refer to the browser window as a whole. For a script in a frame document to replace the entire frameset with a new document, use the following example.

Example

```
top.location.href = "newURL.html"
```

alert()

Displays a dialog box with a message of your choice and gives the user one button to press, OK, which makes the box go away.

Example

```
alert("Don't press that button again. It's too
dangerous.")
```

blur()

Removes focus from the current window.

clearInterval()

This method stops the loop initiated by a `setInterval()`. Use the ID generated by the `setInterval()` method.

Syntax

```
clearInterval(intervalID)
```

clearTimeout()

Stops the time-out delay counter started by a `setTimeout()` method. Use the `timeoutID` to reference the correct time-out counter.

Syntax

```
clearTimeout(timeoutID)
```

close()

Closes the specified window.

Syntax

```
windowReference.close()
```

confirm()

Displays a dialog box with a message of your choice. The user can click one of two buttons: Cancel or OK. If the user clicks Cancel, a Boolean value of `false` is returned. If OK is clicked, `true` is returned.

Example

```
if(confirm("You're really sure you want to send this
form?))
{
    document.forms[0].submit()
}
```

focus()

This shifts focus to the specified window.

open()

Opens a new window. There are many ways to specify parameters for the new window:

copyHistory: Copies the HISTORY object from the current window to the new one.

directories: Displays directory buttons in the new window.

height: Determines the new window's height in pixels.

location: Displays the location field (that is, where you type URLs).

menubar: Displays the menu bar (the menu bar never entirely goes away on a Macintosh, but it's a way to keep someone from reading your source code).

resizable: Allows users to resize the window (which they can always do on a Macintosh, no matter what).

scrollbars: Displays scroll bars if the content is bigger than the window.

status: Displays the status bar in the new window.

toolbar: Displays the tool bar in the new window.

width: Determines the window's width in pixels.

Most of these parameters are specified as either on or off.

Syntax

```
window.open("URL", "windowName", "windowParameters")
```

Example

```
window.open("helpMessage.html", "helper", "height=300,
width=400, location=yes, scrollbars=no, status=no")
```

prompt()

Displays a dialog box with a message, a text field, and two buttons (Cancel and OK). Usually, the message prompts the user to enter some text in the field and click OK. The text the user enters is returned to the script and it's up to your script to deal with the text, if any.

Syntax

```
prompt(message, defaultReply)
```

The `defaultReply` is text that appears in the text field before the user types in anything. Always include this in your script, even if it's an empty string.

Example

```
enteredName = prompt("What's your name?", "")
```

scroll()

Scrolls the document to the specified coordinates.

Syntax

```
scroll(x, y)
```

scrollBy()

Scrolls the document by the number of specified pixels. These values can be positive or negative.

Syntax

```
scrollBy(deltaX, deltaY)
```

setInterval()

Starts a timer that will execute a certain function at intervals you set in the script. The time of the interval between executions is set in milliseconds. This method returns an ID, which is used by the `clearInterval()` method to stop the `setInterval()` loop.

Syntax

```
setInterval(expression/function, msecs)
```

setTimeout()

Starts a nonrepeating timer for a certain number of milliseconds. After that time has elapsed, a specified expression is invoked. When the timer starts, an ID is assigned, so that a `clearTimeout()` method can refer to the ID and stop the `setTimeout()` before all the assigned time has passed. `clearTimeout()` also invokes the expression.

Syntax

```
setTimeout(expression, msecs)
```

frames[]

An array of frames within a certain window. Used to refer to specific frames or windows.

Syntax

```
parent.frames[n]
top.frames[n]
```

Index

A

Absolute coordinates, 55
Absolute position, 5, 54
Active Server Page (ASP), 36, 109
ActiveX controls, 36
Animated product rollout, creation, 49–50
Animation, 40. *See also* Layers, Multiple
          layers, Single layer.
    alternative methods, 54–55
    controls, *See* Direct animation controls.
    timing, 50
    usage, 50
ASP. *See* Active Server Page.

B

Background color, 22, 102, 106
Backtracking, 47
Bitstream fonts, 36
border attribute, 108
Borders, 102, 106
Browsers, 10, 34, 81. *See also* Cross-browser;
          Internet Explorer; Netscape.
    coding, eval( ) usage, 34
    difference, 33
    differences, 61

    stacking, 7
    usage, *See* Overlapping.
Browser-specific features, avoidance, 36

C

Cascading, 16–17
Cascading style sheet (CSS)
    learning, 1
    setup, 42–47
    usage, *See* Homepage.
Cellpadding, 23
Cellspacing, 23
CGI, usage, 109
checkAnswer, 83, 90, 106
checkForm( ), 60
Classes, 12–17. *See also* Tag-bound classes.
    application, 14, 15
    creation, 80
    usage, 16
Clickable images, 8
clickX, 69
clickY, 69
Clipping
    height, 64
    regions, 64–65, 74
    width, 64

Code, process explanation, 4–8, 9–12, 21–23, 27, 30–31, 35–36, 52, 53, 64, 68–73, 80–83; 106. *See also* Draggable layers.
Coding. *See* Browsers; Layer visibility; Style.
Colors, 10, 78. *See also* Background color.
  determination, 12
  names, 9
  setting, 80
Company name, 3, 6, 7
Computer monitors, resolution, 48
Content blocking, DIV usage, 5–6
Control, SPAN usage, 16
Coordinates, 70. *See also* Absolute coordinates; Event coordinate; Negative coordinates.
  measurement, 51
Copyright information, 10, 14
Cross-browser coding, 33, 34
  tricks, 61
Cross-browser DHTML
  coding, 36
  creation, 36
Cross-browser variables, usage, 51
CSS. *See* Cascading style sheet.
currentQuestion, 106, 108
Cursor
  placement, 63
  position, 63

D

Data binding, 36
Davis, Glenn, 83
Design elements, 50
DHTML. *See* Dynamic HyperText Markup Language.
Direct animation controls, 36
DIV tag, 5
  usage, 2, *See also* Content blocking.
Draggable layers, 76
Draggable layers, creation, 57–58
  code, process explanation, 58–73
Dragging, 62–64. *See* Icons; Objects.
  code, 65
  on top, 62–63
dragProduct, 60, 70–72

Dynamic HyperText Markup Language (DHTML), 8, 19, 76, 108
  addition, *See* Homepage DHTML.
  coding, *See* Cross-browser DHTML.
  implementation, 109
  learning, 1
  storefront preparation, 37
  techniques, 31
  usage, *See* Pages.
Dynamically generated pages, 19

E

E-commerce
  page preparation, 38–39
  system, 38
Elements. *See* Form elements.
  positioning, 2–8
  style addition, 8–12
eval( ), 34, 52
  usage, *See* Browsers.
eval( ) statement, 35
  usage, 54
Event coordinate, 63, 64, 69
Events, 58–60. *See also* User events.
  capturing, 68, 74
  handling, 74
  Netscape/MSIE, differences, 61
evt.pageX, 64, 69, 71, 72
evt.pageY, 64, 69, 71, 72

F

Feature image, 30
Feature splash screen, cycling, 27–31
Flash movie, 11
Flash technology (Macromedia), 109
Fonts, 9, 79. *See also* Bitstream fonts; OpenType fonts; Rendered fonts.
  determination, 12
  family, 81
Form elements, 103
Functional spec, 76–78

G

Global variable, 27, 30, 69, 83
Goodman, Danny, 60
grabProduct, 60, 72, 73

H

Header.gif, 3
Headline, 79
Hex values, 10
Homepage, 20, 33, 36
  layout, cascading style sheets,
    usage, 1–2
  navigation, 24
Homepage DHTML
  coding, 33–34
  interactivity, addition, 19–20
HyperText Markup Language (HTML),
    30, 80, 92
  code, 90
  form, 20
HyperText Markup Language (HTML)
    tags, 2, 4
  modification, 8–12

I

Icons, 40, 56. *See also* Page icons; Product.
  dragging, 62
ID selectors, 17
if statement, 70
Images, 103. *See also* Clickable image; Feature
    image; Product; Quiz Progress.
  clicking, 104
  off-screen placement, 54
  overlapping, 7
  placement, 53
  replacement, 30, 102
  transparency, 6, 45
Interactive quiz, 75, 99
  creation, 75–76
  introduction, 99–100
  navigation, 77–78
  progress, 77–78
  results, 78
Interactivity, 57
Internet Explorer (IE), 9, 11, 52, 54, 59
  browsers, 34
  code, 21
  differences, *See* Events; Layers.
  features, avoidance, 36
  syntax, 55, 61, 68
  version 4 browser, 33, 109
Intradocument links, 4

J

Java applets, 36
JavaScript, 19, 30
  backbone creation, 42, 47
  insertion, 34
  memory, 26
  setup, 42–47
  style sheets, 36
  syntax, 33
  usage, *See* Secondary navigation.
JPEG file, 6

K

Kyle, Lynn, 109

L

layer tag, 36
layerRef, 35
Layers. *See* Draggable layers; Moving
    layers; Nested layers;
    Questions; Secondary
    navigation; Shopping cart;
    Sublayers; Text.
  animation, 49, 55, *See also* Multiple
    layers; Single layer.
  creation, *See* Draggable layers.
  dragging, 43, 57–59, 62, 65, 71
  information, 5
  swapping, 28
  usage, 30
  visibility, coding, 35–36
Layers, positioning, 68. *See also* Off-screen
    layers.
  Netscape/MSIE, differences, 61
Line icons. *See* Product.
Links, 14, 24, 100, 107. *See also* Text.
Location, 50, 53
Loop, 51. *See also* while loop.

M

Macromedia. *See* Flash technology.
Margins, 15
Microsoft, standards, 83
Mouse
  clicking, 58, 59, 72
  rollover, 102

MOUSEDOWN, 72
MOUSEMOVE, 72
MOUSEUP, 72
Moving layers, 76
Multiple layers, animation, 52–54

N

Navigation, 101. *See also* Homepage;
    Interactive quiz; Quiz.
  designing, 24
  layer, 26, *See also* Text.
  placement, 22
  pop up, *See* Secondary navigation.
Negative coordinates, 53
Nested layers, 77
Netscape, 9, 11, 52, 54, 59, 60
  browsers, 21, 34
  differences, *See* Events; Layers.
  features, avoidance, 36
  standards, 83
  syntax, 55, 61, 68
nextQuestion, 105

O

Object name, 62
Object/layer, 62
Object-oriented programming, 61
Objects, 61–62
  dragging, 63
  usage, 74
Off-screen layers, positioning, 53–54
offsetX, 69, 71
offsetY, 69, 71
oldLayer, 27
OpenType, 11
OpenType fonts, 36
Overlapping, 16–17
  style, browser usage, 17

P

P tags, 10
padding attribute, 103, 108
Page icons, 77
Pages
  creation, DHTML usage, 38

preparation, *See* E-commerce.
Perl (language), 109
PHP, 109
Pop-up search window, 20–23
Position. *See* Absolute position; Relative
  position.
  definition, STYLE usage, 2–5
Positioning, 51. *See also* Off-screen layers.
Print designers, control, 2
Product
  icon, 42, 49
  image, 62
  line icons, 44
  name, 41
  placement, 57–58
Product rollout
  animation, 42
  creation, *See* Animated product rollout.
Progress. *See* Interactive quiz; Quiz.

Q

Questions. *See* Quiz.
  building, 78–83
  cycling, 83–98
  functionality, 106
  layer, 87
Quiz. *See* Interactive quiz.
  code, 102–106
  conclusion, 106–108
  expectations, 100–102
  navigation, 100–108
  progress, 100–108
    images, 102–106
  questions, 77
Quiz Progress
  image, 106
  section, 100, 102, 105
Quiz Project Chart, 98
quizFinished, 108

R

Relative position, 5, 69
releaseProduct, 60, 73
Rendered fonts, 11
Return statement, 90
Rollout. *See* Animated product rollout.

S

Scoring, 77
Search engine, 20
Search window. *See* Pop-up search
    window.
Secondary navigation, 30
    layers, 26
    pop up, JavaScript usage, 24–27
selectedProduct, 63, 69–72
setTimeout, 52
Shopping cart, 39, 40, 42, 57–58, 73
    area, 41
    information, submitting, 44
    layers, 46
Single layer, animation, 50–52
Site visitors, 39, 42, 52
Space, saving, 84
SPAN tag, 81, 93
    usage, 15, *See also* Control.
Spatial relationship, 62
Splash screen. *See* Feature splash screen.
Stacking. *See* Browsers.
    Z-index usage, 6–8
Storefront
    appearance, 39
    creation, 48
    overview, 39–42
    preparation, *See* Dynamic HyperText
        Markup Language.
Style. *See* Text.
    addition, *See* Elements.
    coding, 85
    conflict, 93
    error, 12
    information, 85
    problem, 78
    usage, 16
STYLE attribute, 17
STYLE tags, 4
    usage, 2, *See also* Position definition.
/STYLE tags, 4
styleRef, 35
Stylesheets, 3, 8, 9, 16, 81
    fundamentals, 1
    layout, 19
    usage, 1, 3, 11

Sublayers, 77
Syntax, 54. *See also* Internet Explorer;
        JavaScript; Netscape.
    usage, 90

T

Table, usage, 81
Tag modifications, 9
Tag-bound classes, 16
Teaser screens, 27
Teaser sequence, 28
testObj, 69, 70
Text, 103
    decorations, 9
    layer, 57
    links, 10
    navigation layer, 13
    style, 78
TrueDoc, 11, 36
tryAgain, 88

U

Underlining, 9
User events, 72
User interface, 62–64, 74
User progression, 101
User system, 79
Utility Functions, 69

V

Variables, 61. *See also* Global variables.
    usage, 56, *See also* Cross-browser
        variables.
VBScript, 36
Visibility. *See* Layers.
Visitors. *See* Site visitors.

W

Web designers, 4, 83
Web pages, 11, 20, 38, 76
Web site, 26, 37, 76, 100, 102, 107
Web Standards Project (WSP), 83
while loop, 106
Whitespace, 70
window.event.srcElement, 70

Workarounds, creation, 81
World Wide Web Consortium, 83
WSP. *See* Web Standards Project.

Z

Z-index, 62, 63, 68
    usage, *See* Stacking.

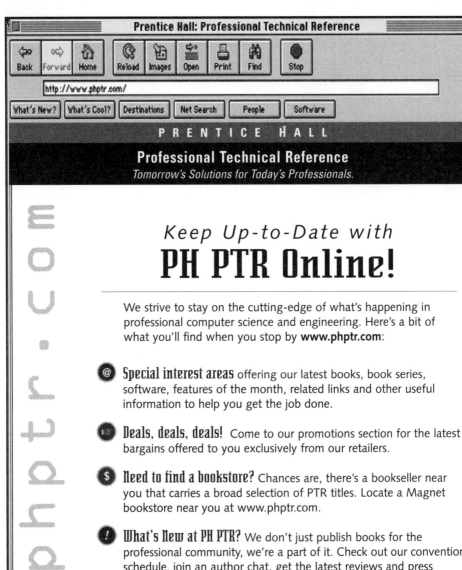